SECURING TELEHEALTH REMOTE PATIENT MONITORING ECOSYSTEM

Healthcare Delivery Organizations (HDOs) are leveraging a combination of telehealth capabilities, such as remote patient monitoring (RPM) and videoconferencing, to treat patients in their homes. These modalities are used to treat numerous conditions, such as patients battling chronic illness or requiring postoperative monitoring. As use of these capabilities continues to grow, it is important to ensure that the infrastructure supporting them can maintain the confidentiality, integrity, and availability of patient data, and to ensure the safety of patients. It is also important to ensure the privacy of patient data by considering the privacy engineering objectives of predictability, manageability, and disassociability of data. The goal of this project is to provide a practical solution for securing the telehealth RPM ecosystem.

NIST encourage technology providers to submit a Letter of Interest should they have a commercially available product suited for the build.

This book includes the Department of Homeland Security document titled: "HIPAA Security Rule Crosswalk to NIST Cybersecurity Framework".

Why buy a book you can download for free?   We print this so you don't have to.

Some are available only in electronic media. Some online docs are missing pages or barely legible.

We at 4th Watch Publishing are former government employees, so we know how government employees actually use the standards. When a new standard is released, an engineer prints it out, punches holes and puts it in a 3-ring binder. While this is not a big deal for a 5 or 10-page document, many NIST documents are over 100 pages and printing a large document is a time-consuming effort. So, an engineer that's paid $75 an hour is spending hours simply printing out the tools needed to do the job. That's time that could be better spent doing engineering. We publish these documents so engineers can focus on what they were hired to do – engineering. It's much more cost-effective to just order the latest version from Amazon.com

If there is a standard you would like published, let us know. Our web site is usgovpub.com

Many of our titles are available as eBooks for Kindle, iPad, Nook, remarkable, BOOX, and Sony eReaders. Buy the paperback from Amazon and get Kindle eBook FREE using MATCHBOOK. Go to https://usgovpub.com to learn more.

Other books we print on Amazon.com

NIST SP 800-66	Implementing the Health Insurance Portability and Accountability Act (HIPAA) Security Rule
NIST SP 1800-1	Securing Electronic Health Records on Mobile Devices
NIST SP 1800-8	Securing Wireless Infusion Pumps
NISTIR 7497	Security Architecture Design Process for Health Information Exchanges (HIEs)
NIST Whitepaper	Securing Telehealth Remote Patient Monitoring Ecosystem

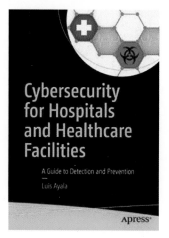

Cybersecurity for Hospitals and Healthcare Facilities: A Guide to Detection and Prevention

Learn how to detect and prevent the hacking of medical equipment at hospitals and healthcare facilities. A cyber-physical attack on building equipment pales in comparison to the damage a determined hacker can do if he/she gains access to a medical-grade network as a medical-grade network controls the diagnostic, treatment, and life support equipment on which lives depend.

 Collins

★★★★★ **Fantastic Cyber Security book on Healthcare**
January 9, 2017
Format: Paperback | Verified Purchase

Great guide for any healthcare practitioner interested in helping secure their infrastructure. The book does a great job setting up the problem currently faced by the healthcare industry to secure the multitude of medical and building internet of things devices inside complex hospital networks. Through each chapter the author hones in on very industry specific best practices form identifying cyber vulnerabilities for remote medical devices to a defined process to securing those devices. Not only is this a great read but there is an appendix is filled with real world procedure templates that can be taken into the field for deployment. Cybersecurity for Hospitals and Healthcare facilitates is a great tool for any healthcare worker interested in learning about cyber-security or a cyber-security practitioner looking to understand the needs of the healthcare industry.

 Jacobs Dad

★★★★★ **Great Foundational Knowledge**
April 17, 2018
Format: Kindle Edition | Verified Purchase

Excellent reference material

SECURING TELEHEALTH REMOTE PATIENT MONITORING ECOSYSTEM

Cybersecurity for the Healthcare Sector

Andrea Arbelaez
National Cybersecurity Center of Excellence
National Institute of Standards and Technology

Ronnie Daldos
Kevin Littlefield
Sue Wang
David Weitzel
The MITRE Corporation

May 2019
hit_nccoe@nist.gov

The National Cybersecurity Center of Excellence (NCCoE), a part of the National Institute of Standards and Technology (NIST), is a collaborative hub where industry organizations, government agencies, and academic institutions work together to address businesses' most pressing cybersecurity challenges. Through this collaboration, the NCCoE develops modular, easily adaptable example cybersecurity solutions demonstrating how to apply standards and best practices using commercially available technology. To learn more about the NCCoE, visit http://www.nccoe.nist.gov. To learn more about NIST, visit http://www.nist.gov.

This document describes a particular problem that is relevant across the healthcare sector. NCCoE cybersecurity experts will address this challenge through collaboration with members of the healthcare sector and vendors of cybersecurity solutions. The resulting reference design will detail an approach that can be used by healthcare delivery organizations (HDOs).

ABSTRACT

HDOs are leveraging a combination of telehealth capabilities, such as remote patient monitoring (RPM) and videoconferencing, to treat patients in their homes. These modalities are used to treat numerous conditions, such as patients battling chronic illness or requiring postoperative monitoring. As use of these capabilities continues to grow, it is important to ensure that the infrastructure supporting them can maintain the confidentiality, integrity, and availability of patient data, and to ensure the safety of patients. It is also important to ensure the privacy of patient data by considering the privacy engineering objectives of predictability, manageability, and disassociability of data. The goal of this project is to provide a practical solution for securing the telehealth RPM ecosystem. The project team will perform a risk assessment on a representative RPM ecosystem in the laboratory environment, apply the NIST Cybersecurity Framework and guidance based on medical device standards, and collaborate with industry and public partners. This project will focus on the diagnostic aspects of remote patient monitoring. The project team will also create a reference design and a detailed description of the practical steps needed to implement a secure solution based on standards and best practices. This project will result in a freely available NIST Cybersecurity Practice Guide.

KEYWORDS

application programming interface; API; application security; cybersecurity; data privacy; data privacy and security risks; health delivery organization; HDO; remote patient monitoring; RPM; telehealth; user interface; UI

DISCLAIMER

TABLE OF CONTENTS

1 Executive Summary..**4**

   Purpose 4

   Scope..4

   Assumptions 5

   Background 5

2 Scenario: Remote Patient Monitoring and Video Telehealth.............................**5**

3 High-Level Architecture **6**

   Component List..8

      Components for RPM Technologies 8

      Components for Remote/Patient Home Environment 8

      Components for HDO Environment 9

      RPM Ecosystem Actors 10

      Desired Security Characteristics...10

4 Relevant Standards and Guidance **12**

   General Cybersecurity and Risk Management 12

   Cybersecurity/Technology-Related Standards 12

   Other Relevant Regulations, Standards, and Guidance (Healthcare/Medical Devices) 13

5 Security Control Map **14**

Appendix A References..**26**

Appendix B Acronyms and Abbreviations..**27**

1 EXECUTIVE SUMMARY

Purpose

This document defines a National Cybersecurity Center of Excellence (NCCoE) project focused on providing guidance and a reference architecture that address security and privacy risks to stakeholders leveraging telehealth and remote patient monitoring (RPM) capabilities.

Health delivery organizations (HDOs) are leveraging a combination of telehealth capabilities, such as RPM and videoconferencing, to treat patients in their homes. Traditionally, patient monitoring systems have been deployed in healthcare facilities, in controlled environments. RPM, however, is different, in that monitoring equipment is deployed in the patient's home, which traditionally does not offer the same level of cybersecurity or physical-security control to prevent misuse or compromise. These RPM devices may use application programming interfaces (APIs) or rule engines developed by third parties that act as intermediaries between the patient and the healthcare provider. Telemetry data from the RPM device may be displayed through a user interface (UI) for visual review.

It is important to review the end-to-end architecture to determine whether security and privacy vulnerabilities exist and what security controls are required for proper cybersecurity of the RPM ecosystem and to protect individuals' privacy.

While the field of telehealth is broad, a focus on the application of telehealth modalities involving telehealth platform providers that use videoconferencing capabilities and leverage cloud and internet technologies coupled with RPM mechanisms provides the NCCoE with an opportunity to develop practical recommendations. The intended audience for these recommendations is HDOs, patients, and independent healthcare providers employing RPM products and services.

This project will result in a publicly available National Institute of Standards and Technology (NIST) Cybersecurity Practice Guide, a detailed implementation guide of the practical steps needed to implement a cybersecurity reference design that addresses this challenge.

Scope

The objective of this project is to demonstrate a proposed approach for improving overall security in the RPM environment. This project will address cybersecurity concerns about having diagnostic monitoring devices in patients' homes, including the home network and patient-owned devices such as smartphones, tablets, laptops, and home computers. This project will also identify cybersecurity measures that HDOs may consider when offering RPM with video telehealth capabilities. A proposed component list is provided in the High-Level Architecture section (Section 3).

Telehealth solutions are, by nature, an integration of disparate parties and environments. However, out of scope for this project are the risks and concerns specific to the third-party provider (i.e., the telehealth platform provider) that may offer services that are cloud-hosted or that provide functionality through a software-as-a-service model. Additionally, this project does not evaluate monitoring devices for vulnerabilities, flaws, or defects. This project will focus on the medical diagnostic aspects of remote patient monitoring. The NCCoE does not evaluate medical device manufacturers.

While telehealth solutions may include software development kits (SDKs) and APIs, this project will not explore the secure software development practice in detail.

Assumptions

- Patient monitoring devices (e.g., blood pressure cuffs, body mass index [BMI]/weight scales) may leverage commercially available communications (e.g., Bluetooth, Wi-Fi/wireless, or cellular) to transmit telemetry data to the home monitoring application.
- The home monitoring application is a provider-managed solution that may be installed on a provider-managed or unmanaged patient-owned mobile device.
- The home monitoring application may transmit telemetry data to the remote monitoring server via a cellular or Wi-Fi connection.
- The patient is in his or her home during the telehealth interaction (e.g., video, patient monitoring).
- Video telehealth interactions may leverage patient-owned devices or devices provided by the primary care facility.
- Clinicians participating in telehealth interactions use secured communications methods.

Background

The NCCoE recognizes the important role that telehealth capabilities play in delivery of healthcare and has commenced research in telehealth, specifically RPM technologies. As the growth and popularity of telehealth capabilities accelerate, it is critical to evaluate the security and privacy risks associated with each identified use case. Once identified, security controls can be implemented to mitigate the security and privacy risks to the patient and other stakeholders. The demand for telehealth capabilities continues to grow as stakeholders (e.g., patients; providers; payers; federal, state, and local governments) see the benefits that telehealth brings to improving the quality of patient care and the accessibility to healthcare. As an example of telehealth capabilities growth, a 2017 Foley Telemedicine and Digital Health Survey found that, in just three years, respondents went from 87 percent not expecting most of their patients to be using telehealth services in 2017 to 75 percent offering or planning to offer telehealth services to their patients [1].

This project examines RPM as a medically prescriptive course that an HDO implements to manage a condition outside a healthcare facility. This differs from discretionary use of personal healthcare technology that individuals may use in improving their fitness.

2 SCENARIO: REMOTE PATIENT MONITORING AND VIDEO TELEHEALTH

The scenario considered for this project involves RPM equipment deployed to the patient's home [2]. RPM equipment that may be provided to patients includes devices for blood pressure monitoring, heart rate monitoring, BMI/weight measurements, and glucose monitoring. An accompanying application may also be downloaded onto the patient-owned device and synced with the RPM equipment to enable the patient and healthcare provider to share data. Patients may also be able to initiate videoconferencing and/or communicate with the healthcare provider via email, text messaging, chat sessions, or voice communication. Data may be transmitted across the patient's home network and routed across the public internet. Those transmissions may be relayed to a telehealth platform provider that, in turn, routes the communications to the HDO. This process brings the patient and healthcare provider together, allowing for delivery of the needed healthcare services in the comfort of the patient's home.

The following functions may be evaluated during this project:

- connectivity between monitoring devices and applications deployed to mobile devices (e.g., smartphones, tablets) or to patient workstations (e.g., laptops, desktops)
- ability for the application to transmit monitoring data to the HDO
- ability for the patient to initiate requests or notifications
- ability for the patient to interact with a point of contact to initiate care (This ability may be through a chat box, interacting with a live individual via videoconference.)
- ability for the patient to receive medical alerts and notifications
- ability for the monitoring data to be analyzed by the HDO to spot trends and to issue possible alerts to the clinician if the data suggests that there is an issue with the patient
- ability for the patient monitoring data to be shared remotely with the electronic health record system
- ability for the patient to initiate a videoconference session with a care team member through the telehealth application
- ability for the HDO to update the security functionality of the remote monitoring device
- ability for the patient to receive and apply security updates and patches for applications
- ability for the HDO to connect to the remote monitoring device to obtain direct patient telemetry data
- ability for the HDO to connect to the remote monitoring device to update the monitoring device configuration

3 HIGH-LEVEL ARCHITECTURE

This project examines what happens when remote patient monitoring equipment is hosted in a patient's home environment. Patients who use monitoring devices in their home are able to forward the monitoring data to their physician at regular intervals and can initiate audio and video communication to their care team providers. Physicians receive patient data through the telehealth platform with equipment that captures the patient data and allows real-time audio and video interaction with the patient. This project identifies controls in the HDO environment with a focus on patient home-deployed controls.

For this project, two separate environments will be constructed: the HDO environment and the patient home setting. Figure 3-1 shows the high-level architecture for RPM that uses a third-party telehealth platform provider. The high-level architecture addresses the scope noted in Section 1. The component list and the desired security characteristics are listed in the subsections that follow.

The HDO infrastructure would adopt the deployments used in previous NCCoE healthcare projects [3], [4] that implement network zoning and layered defenses aligning to NIST Cybersecurity Framework functions. As this project develops, identity and access management (IdAM) controls will be identified. IdAM may be limited based on selected technologies, and those limitations are to be determined.

Figure 3-1: High-Level Architecture

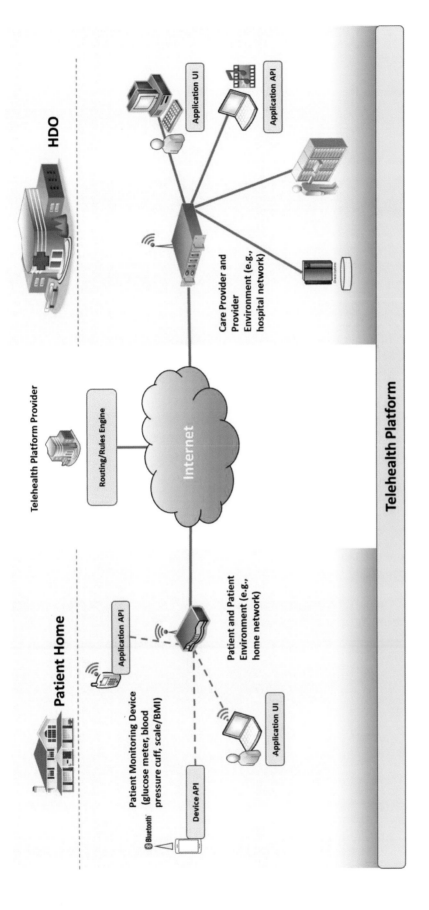

Component List

The NCCoE has a dedicated lab environment that includes the following features:

- network with machines using a directory service
- virtualization servers
- network switches
- remote access solution with Wi-Fi and a virtual private network (VPN)

Collaboration partners (participating vendors) may provide specialized components and capabilities to realize this solution, including, but not limited to, those listed in the subsections below.

Components for RPM Technologies

- **telehealth platform**–a solution that enables data and communication flow from the patient monitoring device to the home monitoring device to the care providers
    - internet-based communications
        - transmission of telemetry data
        - videoconference
        - audioconference
        - email
        - secure text messaging
    - routing/triage functionality–The telehealth platform enables patients to identify an appropriate, networked team of care providers.
    - SDKs and APIs that enable telehealth applications to interface with patient monitoring devices
    - patient monitoring devices that send telemetry data via the home monitoring device
        - blood pressure
        - heart monitoring
        - BMI/weight scales
        - other telemetry devices, as appropriate
    - home monitoring device (e.g., specialized mobile application, stand-alone device) that transmits telemetry data to the telehealth platform and provides video connectivity

Components for Remote/Patient Home Environment

- **personal firewall**–an application that controls network traffic to and from a computer, permitting or denying communications based on a security policy
- **wireless access point router**–a device that performs the functions of a router and includes the functions of a wireless access point
- **endpoint protection (anti-malware)**–a type of software program designed to prevent, detect, and remove malicious software (malware) on information technology (IT) systems and on individual computing devices
- **mobile device**–a multimodal, small form factor, communications mechanism that has characteristics of computing devices that include wireless network capability, memory,

data storage, and processing. The device may provide real-time audio, video, and text communications as well as support email, web browsing, and other internet-enabled methods to interact with locally and remotely stored information and systems.

- **modem**–a device that provides a demarcation point for broadband communications access (e.g., cable, digital subscriber line [DSL], wireless, long-term-evolution [LTE], 5G) and presents an Ethernet interface to allow internet access via the broadband infrastructure
- **wireless router**–a device that provides wireless connectivity to the home network and provides access to the internet via a connection to the cable modem
- **telehealth application**–an application residing on a managed or unmanaged mobile device or on a specialized stand-alone device and that facilitates transmission of telemetry data and video connectivity between the patient and HDO
- **patient monitoring device**–a peripheral device used by the patient to perform diagnostic tasks (e.g., measure blood pressure, glucose levels, or BMI/weight) and to send the telemetry data via Bluetooth or wireless connectivity to the telehealth application

Components for HDO Environment

- **network access control**–discovers and accurately identifies devices connected to wired networks, wireless networks, and VPNs and provides network access controls to ensure that only authorized individuals with authorized devices can access the systems and data that access policy permits
- **network firewall**–a network security device that monitors and controls incoming and outgoing network traffic, based on defined security rules
- **intrusion detection system (IDS) (host/network)**–a device or software application that monitors a network or systems for malicious activity or policy violations
- **intrusion prevention system (IPS)**–a device that monitors network traffic and can take immediate action, such as shutting down a port, based on a set of rules established by the network administrator
- **VPN**–a secure endpoint access solution that delivers secure remote access through virtual private networking
- **governance, risk, and compliance (GRC) tool**–automated management for an organization's overall governance, enterprise risk management, and compliance with regulations
- **network management tool**–provides server, application-management, and monitoring services, as well as asset life-cycle management
- **endpoint protection and security**–provides server hardening, protection, monitoring, and workload micro-segmentation for private cloud and physical on-premises data-center environments, along with support for containers, and provides full-disk and removable media encryption
- **anti-ransomware**–helps enterprises defend against ransomware attacks by exposing, detecting, and quarantining advanced and evasive ransomware
- **application security scanning/testing**–provides a means for custom application code testing (static/dynamic)

- **patients**–individuals being monitored in their home settings
- **HDO clinicians**–physicians, nursing staff, and medical technicians in the HDO environment
- **independent healthcare providers**–those who may need to access patient information for patient-initiated care and diagnostic requests
- **support/maintenance staff**–technical staff in the HDO facility who maintain the HDO-resident components and the HDO-managed components in the patient's home environment

Desired Security Characteristics

The primary security functions and processes to be implemented for this project are listed below and are based on NIST Cybersecurity Framework Version 1.1.

IDENTIFY (ID)–*These activities are foundational to developing an organizational understanding to manage risk.*

- **asset management**–includes identification and management of assets on the network and management of the assets to be deployed to equipment. Implementation of this category may vary depending on the parties managing the equipment. However, this category remains relevant as a fundamental component in establishing appropriate cybersecurity practices.
- **governance**–Organizational cybersecurity policy is established and communicated. Governance practices are appropriate for HDOs and their solution partners, including technology providers and those vendors that develop, support, and operate telehealth platforms.
- **risk assessment**–includes the risk management strategy. Risk assessment is a fundamental component for HDOs and their solution partners.
- **supply chain risk management**–The nature of telehealth with RPM is that the system integrates components sourced from disparate vendors and may involve relationships established with multiple suppliers, including cloud services providers.

PROTECT (PR)–*These activities support the ability to develop and implement appropriate safeguards based on risk.*

- **identity management, authentication, and access control**–includes user account management and remote access
  - controlling (and auditing) user accounts
  - controlling (and auditing) access by external users
  - enforcing least privilege for all (internal and external) users
  - enforcing separation-of-duties policies
    - privileged access management (PAM) with an emphasis on separation of duties
  - enforcing least functionality
- **data security**–includes data confidentiality, integrity, and availability
  - securing and monitoring storage of data–includes data encryption (for data at rest)

- access control on data
- data-at-rest controls should implement some form of a data security manager that would allow for policy application to encrypt data, inclusive of access control policy
  - securing distribution of data–includes data encryption (for data in transit) and a data loss prevention mechanism
  - controls that promote data integrity
  - Cryptographic modules validated as meeting NIST Federal Information Processing Standards (FIPS) 140-2 are preferred.
- **information protection processes and procedures**–include data backup and endpoint protection
- **maintenance**–includes local and remote maintenance
- **protective technology**–host-based intrusion prevention, solutions for malware (malicious-code detection), audit logging, (automated) audit log review, and physical protection

DETECT (DE)–*These activities enable timely discovery of a cybersecurity event.*

- **security continuous monitoring**–monitoring for unauthorized personnel, devices, software, and connections
  - vulnerability management–includes vulnerability scanning and remediation
  - patch management
  - system configuration security settings
  - user account usage (local and remote) and user behavioral analytics
  - security log analysis

RESPOND (RS)–*These activities support development and implementation of actions designed to contain the impact of a detected cybersecurity event.*

- **response planning**–Response processes and procedures are executed and maintained to ensure a response to a detected cybersecurity incident.
- **mitigation**–Activities are performed to prevent expansion of a cybersecurity event, mitigate its effects, and resolve the incident.

RECOVER (RC)–*These activities support development and implementation of actions for the timely recovery of normal operations after a cybersecurity incident.*

- **recovery planning**–Recovery processes and procedures are executed and maintained to ensure restoration of systems or assets affected by cybersecurity incidents.
- **communications**–Restoration activities are coordinated with internal and external parties (e.g., coordinating centers, internet service providers, owners of attacking systems, victims, other computer security incident response teams, vendors).

4 RELEVANT STANDARDS AND GUIDANCE

General Cybersecurity and Risk Management

- Association for Advancement of Medical Instrumentation (AAMI) Technical Information Report 57, *Principles for medical device security–Risk management*
- Department of Health and Human Services (HHS), "The HIPAA Privacy Rule," https://www.hhs.gov/hipaa/for-professionals/privacy/index.html
- HHS, "The HIPAA Security Rule," https://www.hhs.gov/hipaa/for-professionals/security/index.html
- International Organization for Standardization (ISO)/International Electrotechnical Commission (IEC) Standard 27001:2013, *Information technology–Security techniques–Information security management systems–Requirements*
- American National Standards Institute/AAMI/IEC Standard 80001-1:2010, *Application of risk management for IT-networks incorporating medical devices–Part 1: Roles, responsibilities and activities*
- IEC Technical Report (TR) 80001-2-1 Edition 1.0 2012-07, *Application of risk management for IT-networks incorporating medical devices–Part 2-1: Step-by-step risk management of medical IT-networks–Practical applications and examples*
- IEC TR 80001-2-2 Edition 1.0 2012-07, *Application of risk management for IT-networks incorporating medical devices–Part 2-2: Guidance for the disclosure and communication of medical device security needs, risks and controls*
- NIST Cybersecurity Framework Version 1.1, "Framework for Improving Critical Infrastructure Cybersecurity," https://www.nist.gov/cyberframework/framework
- NIST Interagency/Internal Report 8062, *An Introduction to Privacy Engineering and Risk Management in Federal Systems,* https://csrc.nist.gov/publications/detail/nistir/8062/final
- NIST Special Publication (SP) 800-30 Revision 1, *Guide for Conducting Risk Assessments,* http://nvlpubs.nist.gov/nistpubs/Legacy/SP/nistspecialpublication800-30r1.pdf
- NIST SP 800-37 Revision 2, *Risk Management Framework for Information Systems and Organizations: A System Life Cycle Approach for Security and Privacy,* https://csrc.nist.gov/publications/detail/sp/800-37/rev-2/final
- NIST SP 800-39, *Managing Information Security Risk: Organization, Mission, and Information System View,* http://nvlpubs.nist.gov/nistpubs/Legacy/SP/nistspecialpublication800-39.pdf
- NIST SP 800-53 Revision 4, *Security and Privacy Controls for Federal Information Systems and Organizations,* http://nvlpubs.nist.gov/nistpubs/SpecialPublications/NIST.SP.800-53r4.pdf

Cybersecurity/Technology-Related Standards

- NIST Interagency/Internal Report 8228 Draft, *Considerations for Managing Internet of Things (IOT) Cybersecurity and Privacy Risks,* https://doi.org/10.6028/NIST.IR.8228-draft
- NIST FIPS 140-2, *Security Requirements for Cryptographic Modules,* https://csrc.nist.gov/publications/detail/fips/140/2/final

- NIST SP 800-41 Revision 1, *Guidelines on Firewalls and Firewall Policy,*
  http://nvlpubs.nist.gov/nistpubs/Legacy/SP/nistspecialpublication800-41r1.pdf
- NIST SP 800-52 Revision 1, *Guidelines for the Selection, Configuration, and Use of Transport Layer Security (TLS) Implementations,*
  http://nvlpubs.nist.gov/nistpubs/SpecialPublications/NIST.SP.800-52r1.pdf
- NIST SP 800-57 Part 1 Revision 4, *Recommendation for Key Management: Part 1: General,*
  http://nvlpubs.nist.gov/nistpubs/SpecialPublications/NIST.SP.800-57pt1r4.pdf
- NIST SP 800-77, *Guide to IPsec VPNs,*
  http://nvlpubs.nist.gov/nistpubs/Legacy/SP/nistspecialpublication800-77.pdf
- NIST SP 800-95, *Guide to Secure Web Services,*
  http://nvlpubs.nist.gov/nistpubs/Legacy/SP/nistspecialpublication800-95.pdf
- NIST SP 800-121 Revision 2, *Guide to Bluetooth Security,*
  https://nvlpubs.nist.gov/nistpubs/SpecialPublications/NIST.SP.800-121r2.pdf
- NIST SP 800-144, *Guidelines on Security and Privacy in Public Cloud Computing,*
  http://nvlpubs.nist.gov/nistpubs/Legacy/SP/nistspecialpublication800-144.pdf
- NIST SP 800-146, *Cloud Computing Synopsis and Recommendations,*
  http://nvlpubs.nist.gov/nistpubs/Legacy/SP/nistspecialpublication800-146.pdf
- NIST SP 1800-1, *Securing Electronic Health Records on Mobile Devices,*
  https://csrc.nist.gov/publications/detail/sp/1800-1/final

Other Relevant Regulations, Standards, and Guidance (Healthcare/Medical Devices)

- Department of Health and Human Services Office for Civil Rights, "HIPAA Security Rule Crosswalk to NIST Cybersecurity Framework,"
  https://www.hhs.gov/sites/default/files/nist-csf-to-hipaa-security-rule-crosswalk-02-22-2016-final.pdf
- Department of Homeland Security, National Cybersecurity and Communications Integration Center, "Attack Surface: Healthcare and Public Health Sector,"
  https://info.publicintelligence.net/NCCIC-MedicalDevices.pdf
- Food and Drug Administration (FDA), "Content of Premarket Submissions for Management of Cybersecurity in Medical Devices Guidance" (revision in Draft),
  https://www.fda.gov/downloads/MedicalDevices/DeviceRegulationandGuidance/GuidanceDocuments/UCM623529.pdf
- FDA, "Radio Frequency Wireless Technology in Medical Devices—Guidance for Industry and FDA Staff,"
  https://www.fda.gov/downloads/MedicalDevices/DeviceRegulationandGuidance/GuidanceDocuments/UCM077272.pdf
- FDA, "Content of Premarket Submissions for Management of Cybersecurity in Medical Devices: Guidance for Industry and Food and Drug Administration Staff,"
  https://www.fda.gov/downloads/medicaldevices/deviceregulationandguidance/guidancedocuments/ucm356190.pdf
- FDA, "Guidance for Industry: Cybersecurity for Networked Medical Devices Containing Off-the-Shelf (OTS) Software,"

https://www.fda.gov/downloads/MedicalDevices/DeviceRegulationandGuidance/GuidanceDocuments/UCM077823.pdf

- FDA, "Postmarket Management of Cybersecurity in Medical Devices: Guidance for Industry and Food and Drug Administration Staff," https://www.fda.gov/regulatory-information/search-fda-guidance-documents/postmarket-management-cybersecurity-medical-devices

- NIST SP 800-66 Revision 1, *An Introductory Resource Guide for Implementing the Health Insurance Portability and Accountability Act (HIPAA) Security Rule,* http://nvlpubs.nist.gov/nistpubs/Legacy/SP/nistspecialpublication800-66r1.pdf

5 SECURITY CONTROL MAP

Table 5-1 maps the characteristics of the commercial products that the NCCoE will apply to this cybersecurity challenge to the applicable standards and best practices described in the Framework for Improving Critical Infrastructure Cybersecurity (NIST Cybersecurity Framework) and to healthcare-specific standards and guidance, such as IEC TR 80001-2-2, HIPAA, and ISO/IEC 27001. This exercise is meant to demonstrate the real-world applicability of standards and best practices but does not imply that products with these characteristics will meet an industry's requirements for regulatory approval or accreditation.

Table 5-1: Security Control Map

NIST Cybersecurity Framework Version 1.1				Sector-Specific Standards and Best Practices		
Function	Category	Subcategory	NIST SP 800-53 Revision 4	IEC TR 80001-2-2	HIPAA Security Rule	ISO/IEC 27001
IDENTIFY (ID)	Asset Management (ID.AM)	ID.AM-1: Physical devices and systems within the organization are inventoried.	CM-8	Not applicable	45 C.F.R. §§ 164.308(a)(1)(ii)(A), 164.310(a)(2)(ii), 164.310(d)	A.8.1.1, A.8.1.2
		ID.AM-5: Resources (e.g., hardware, devices, data, time, and software) are prioritized based on their classification, criticality, and business value.	CP-2, RA-2, SA-14	DTBK	45 C.F.R. § 164.308(a)(7)(ii)(E)	A.8.2.1
	Risk Assessment (ID.RA)	ID.RA-1: Asset vulnerabilities are identified and documented.	CA-2, CA-7, CA-8, RA-3, RA-5, SA-5, SA-11, SI-2, SI-4, SI-5	RDMP	45 C.F.R. §§ 164.308(a)(1)(ii)(A), 164.308(a)(7)(ii)(E), 164.308(a)(8), 164.310(a)(1), 164.312(a)(1), 164.316(b)(2)(iii)	A.12.6.1, A.18.2.3
		ID.RA-4: Potential business impacts and likelihoods are identified.	RA-2, RA-3, PM-9, PM-11, SA-14	SAHD, SGUD	45 C.F.R. §§ 164.308(a)(1)(i), 164.308(a)(1)(ii)(A), 164.308(a)(1)(ii)(B), 164.308(a)(6), 164.308(a)(7)(ii)(E), 164.308(a)(8), 164.316(a)	A.12.6.1, A.18.2.3

NIST Cybersecurity Framework Version 1.1				Sector-Specific Standards and Best Practices		
Function	Category	Subcategory	NIST SP 800-53 Revision 4	IEC TR 80001-2-2	HIPAA Security Rule	ISO/IEC 27001
		ID.RA-5: Threats, vulnerabilities, likelihoods, and impacts are used to determine risk.	RA-2, RA-3, PM-16	SGUD	45 C.F.R. §§ 164.308(a)(1)(ii)(A), 164.308(a)(1)(ii)(B), 164.308(a)(1)(ii)(D), 164.308(a)(7)(ii)(D), 164.308(a)(7)(ii)(E), 164.316(a)	None
		ID.RA-6: Risk responses are identified and prioritized.	PM-4, PM-9	DTBK, SGUD	45 C.F.R. §§ 164.308(a)(1)(ii)(B), 164.314(a)(2)(i)(C), 164.314(b)(2)(iv)	None
		(Note: not directly mapped in Cybersecurity Framework)	AC-1, AC-11, AC-12	ALOF	Not applicable	None
PROTECT (PR)	Identity Management and Access Control (PR.AC)	PR.AC-1: Identities and credentials are issued, managed, revoked, and audited for authorized devices, users, and processes.	AC-2, IA Family	AUTH, CNFS, EMRG, PAUT	45 C.F.R. §§ 164.308(a)(3)(ii)(B), 164.308(a)(3)(ii)(C), 164.308(a)(4)(i), 164.308(a)(4)(ii)(B), 164.308(a)(4)(ii)(C), 164.312(a)(2)(i), 164.312(a)(2)(ii), 164.312(a)(2)(iii), 164.312(d)	A.9.2.1, A.9.2.2, A.9.2.4, A.9.3.1, A.9.4.2, A.9.4.3

NIST Cybersecurity Framework Version 1.1			NIST SP 800-53 Revision 4	Sector-Specific Standards and Best Practices		
Function	Category	Subcategory		IEC TR 80001-2-2	HIPAA Security Rule	ISO/IEC 27001
		PR.AC-2: Physical access to assets is managed and protected.	PE-2, PE-3, PE-4, PE-5, PE-6, PE-9	PLOK, TXCF, TXIG	45 C.F.R. §§ 164.308(a)(1)(ii)(B), 164.308(a)(7)(i), 164.308(a)(7)(ii)(A), 164.310(a)(1), 164.310(a)(2)(i), 164.310(a)(2)(ii), 164.310(a)(2)(iii), 164.310(b), 164.310(c), 164.310(d)(1), 164.310(d)(2)(iii)	A.11.1.1, A.11.1.2, A.11.1.4, A.11.1.6, A.11.2.3
		PR.AC-3: Remote access is managed.	AC-17, AC-19, AC-20	NAUT, PAUT	45 C.F.R. §§ 164.308(a)(4)(i), 164.308(b)(1), 164.308(b)(3), 164.310(b), 164.312(e)(1), 164.312(e)(2)(ii)	A.6.2.2, A.13.1.1, A.13.2.1
		PR.AC-4: Access permissions and authorizations are managed, incorporating the principles of least privilege and separation of duties.	AC-2, AC-3, AC-5, AC-6, AC-16	AUTH, CNFS, EMRG, NAUT, PAUT	45 C.F.R. §§ 164.308(a)(3), 164.308(a)(4), 164.310(a)(2)(iii), 164.310(b), 164.312(a)(1), 164.312(a)(2)(i), 164.312(a)(2)(ii)	A.6.1.2, A.9.1.2, A.9.2.3, A.9.4.1, A.9.4.4

NIST Cybersecurity Framework Version 1.1				Sector-Specific Standards and Best Practices		
Function	Category	Subcategory	NIST SP 800-53 Revision 4	IEC TR 80001-2-2	HIPAA Security Rule	ISO/IEC 27001
		PR.AC-5: Network integrity is protected, incorporating network segregation where appropriate.	AC-4, SC-7	NAUT	45 C.F.R. §§ 164.308(a)(4)(ii)(B), 164.310(a)(1), 164.310(b), 164.312(a)(1), 164.312(b), 164.312(c), 164.312(e)	A.13.1.1, A.13.1.3, A.13.2.1
		PR.AC-6: Identities are proofed and bound to credentials and asserted in interactions when appropriate.	AC-2, AC-3, AC-5, AC-6, AC-16, AC-19, AC-24, IA-2, IA-4, IA-5, IA-8, PE-2, PS-3	AUTH, CNFS, EMRG, NAUT, PLOK, SGUD	Not applicable	A.6.1.2, A.9.1.2, A.9.2.2, A.9.2.3, A.9.2.5, A.9.2.6, A.9.4.1, A.9.4.4
	Data Security (PR.DS)	PR.DS-1: Data at rest is protected.	SC-28	IGAU, STCF	45 C.F.R. §§ 164.308(a)(1)(ii)(D), 164.308(b)(1), 164.310(d), 164.312(a)(1), 164.312(a)(2)(iii), 164.312(a)(2)(iv), 164.312(b), 164.312(c), 164.312(d), 164.314(b)(2)(i)	A.8.2.3

NIST Cybersecurity Framework Version 1.1			NIST SP 800-53 Revision 4	Sector-Specific Standards and Best Practices		
Function	Category	Subcategory		IEC TR 80001-2-2	HIPAA Security Rule	ISO/IEC 27001
		PR.DS-2: Data in transit is protected.	SC-8	IGAU, TXCF	45 C.F.R. §§ 164.308(b)(1), 164.308(b)(2), 164.312(e)(1), 164.312(e)(2)(i), 164.312(e)(2)(ii), 164.314(b)(2)(i)	A.8.2.3, A.13.1.1, A.13.2.1, A.13.2.3, A.14.1.2, A.14.1.3
		PR.DS-3: Assets are formally managed throughout removal, transfers, and disposition.	CM-8, MP-6, PE-16	Not applicable	45 C.F.R. §§ 164.308(a)(1)(ii)(A), 164.310(a)(2)(ii), 164.310(a)(2)(iii), 164.310(a)(2)(iv), 164.310(d)(1), 164.310(d)(2)	A.12.3.1
		PR.DS-4: Adequate capacity to ensure availability is maintained.	AU-4, CP-2, SC-5	AUDT, DTBK	45 C.F.R. §§ 164.308(a)(1)(ii)(A), 164.308(a)(1)(ii)(B), 164.308(a)(7), 164.310(a)(2)(i), 164.310(d)(2)(iv), 164.312(a)(2)(ii)	A.12.3.1

| NIST Cybersecurity Framework Version 1.1 | | | | Sector-Specific Standards and Best Practices | | |
Function	Category	Subcategory	NIST SP 800-53 Revision 4	IEC TR 80001-2-2	HIPAA Security Rule	ISO/IEC 27001
		PR.DS-5: Protections against data leaks are implemented.	AC-4, AC-5, AC-6, PE-19, PS-3, PS-6, SC-7, SC-8, SC-13, SC-31, SI-4	AUTH, CNFS, STCF, TXCF, TXIG	45 C.F.R. §§ 164.308(a)(1)(ii)(D), 164.308(a)(3), 164.308(a)(4), 164.310(b), 164.310(c), 164.312(a), 164.312(e)	A.6.1.2, A.7.1.1, A.7.1.2, A.7.3.1, A.8.2.2, A.8.2.3, A.9.1.1, A.9.1.2, A.9.2.3, A.9.4.1, A.9.4.4, A.9.4.5, A.13.1.3, A.13.2.1, A.13.2.3, A.13.2.4, A.14.1.2, A.14.1.3
		PR.DS-6: Integrity checking mechanisms are used to verify software, firmware, and information integrity.	SI-7	IGAU	45 C.F.R. §§ 164.308(a)(1)(ii)(D), 164.312(b), 164.312(c)(1), 164.312(c)(2), 164.312(e)(2)(i)	A.12.2.1, A.12.5.1, A.14.1.2, A.14.1.3
		PR.DS-7: The development and testing environment(s) are separate from the production environment.	CM-2	CNFS	45 C.F.R. § 164.308(a)(4)	A.12.1.4
	Information Protection Processes and Procedures (PR.IP)	PR.IP-4: Backups of information are conducted, maintained, and tested periodically.	CP-4, CP-6, CP-9	DTBK	45 C.F.R. §§ 164.308(a)(7)(ii)(A), 164.308(a)(7)(ii)(B), 164.308(a)(7)(ii)(D), 164.310(a)(2)(i), 164.310(d)(2)(iv)	A.12.3.1, A.17.1.2, A.17.1.3, A.18.1.3

NIST Cybersecurity Framework Version 1.1				Sector-Specific Standards and Best Practices		
Function	Category	Subcategory	NIST SP 800-53 Revision 4	IEC TR 80001-2-2	HIPAA Security Rule	ISO/IEC 27001
		PR.IP-6: Data is destroyed according to policy.	MP-6	DIDT	45 C.F.R. §§ 164.310(d)(2)(i), 164.310(d)(2)(ii)	A.8.2.3, A.8.3.1, A.8.3.2, A.11.2.7
		PR.IP-9: Response plans (Incident Response and Business Continuity) and recovery plans (Incident Recovery and Disaster Recovery) are in place and managed.	CP-2, IR-8	DTBK	45 C.F.R. §§ 164.308(a)(6), 164.308(a)(7), 164.310(a)(2)(i), 164.312(a)(2)(ii)	A.16.1.1, A.17.1.1, A.17.1.2
		PR.IP-10: Response and recovery plans are tested.	CP-4, IR-3, PM-14	DTBK	45 C.F.R. § 164.308(a)(7)(ii)(D)	A.17.1.3
		PR.IP-12: A vulnerability management plan is developed and implemented.	RA-3, RA-5, SI-2	MLDP	45 C.F.R. §§ 164.308(a)(1)(i), 164.308(a)(1)(ii)(A), 164.308(a)(1)(ii)(B)	A.12.6.1, A.18.2.2
	Maintenance (PR.MA)	PR.MA-1: Maintenance and repair of organizational assets is performed and logged in a timely manner, with approved and controlled tools.	MA-2, MA-3, MA-5	CSUP, RDMP	45 C.F.R. §§ 164.308(a)(3)(ii)(A), 164.310(a)(2)(iv)	A.11.1.2, A.11.2.4, A.11.2.5

NIST Cybersecurity Framework Version 1.1				Sector-Specific Standards and Best Practices		
Function	Category	Subcategory	NIST SP 800-53 Revision 4	IEC TR 80001-2-2	HIPAA Security Rule	ISO/IEC 27001
		PR.MA-2: Remote maintenance of organizational assets is approved, logged, and performed in a manner that prevents unauthorized access.	MA-4	CSUP	45 C.F.R. §§ 164.308(a)(1)(ii)(D), 164.308(a)(3)(ii)(A), 164.310(d)(1), 164.310(d)(2)(ii), 164.310(d)(2)(iii), 164.312(a), 164.312(a)(2)(ii), 164.312(a)(2)(iv), 164.312(b), 164.312(d), 164.312(e)	A.11.2.4, A.15.1.1, A.15.2.1
		PR.PT-1: Audit/log records are determined, documented, implemented, and reviewed in accordance with policy.	AC-4, AC-17, AC-18, CP-8, SC-7	AUDT	45 C.F.R. §§ 164.308(a)(1)(ii)(D), 164.308(a)(5)(ii)(C), 164.310(a)(2)(iv), 164.310(d)(2)(iii), 164.312(b)	A.12.4.1, A.12.4.2, A.12.4.3, A.12.4.4, A.12.7.1
	Protective Technology (PR.PT)	PR.PT-3: The principle of least functionality is incorporated by configuring systems to provide only essential capabilities.	AC-3, CM-7	AUTH, CNFS	45 C.F.R. §§ 164.308(a)(3), 164.308(a)(4), 164.310(a)(2)(iii), 164.310(b), 164.310(c), 164.312(a)(1), 164.312(a)(2)(i), 164.312(a)(2)(ii), 164.312(a)(2)(iv)	A.9.1.2

NIST Cybersecurity Framework Version 1.1				Sector-Specific Standards and Best Practices		
Function	Category	Subcategory	NIST SP 800-53 Revision 4	IEC TR 80001-2-2	HIPAA Security Rule	ISO/IEC 27001
		PR.PT-4: Communications and control networks are protected.	AC-4, AC-17, AC-18, CP-8, SC-7	DTBK	45 C.F.R. §§ 164.308(a)(1)(ii)(D), 164.312(a)(1), 164.312(b), 164.312(e)	A.13.1.1, A.13.2.1
DETECT (DE)	Anomalies and Events (DE.AE)	DE.AE-1: A baseline of network operations and expected data flows for users and systems is established and managed.	AC-4, CA-3, CM-2, SI-4	AUTH, CNFS	45 C.F.R. §§ 164.308(a)(1)(ii)(D), 164.312(b)	None
		DE.AE-2: Detected events are analyzed to understand attack targets and methods.	CP-2, IR-4, RA-3, SI-4	DTBK	45 C.F.R. § 164.308(6)(i)	A.16.1.1, A.16.1.4
	Security Continuous Monitoring (DE.CM)	DE.CM-1: The network is monitored to detect potential cybersecurity events.	AC-2, AU-12, CA-7, CM-3, SC-5, SC-7, SI-4	AUTH, CNFS, EMRG, MLDP	45 C.F.R. §§ 164.308(a)(1)(ii)(D), 164.308(a)(5)(ii)(B), 164.308(a)(5)(ii)(C), 164.308(a)(8), 164.312(b), 164.312(e)(2)(i)	None
		DE.CM-2: The physical environment is monitored to detect potential cybersecurity events.	CA-7, PE-3, PE-6, PE-20	MLDP	45 C.F.R. §§ 164.310(a)(2)(ii), 164.310(a)(2)(iii)	None
		DE.CM-4: Malicious code is detected.	SI-3	IGAU, MLDP, TXIG	45 C.F.R. §§ 164.308(a)(1)(ii)(D), 164.308(a)(5)(ii)(B)	A.12.2.1

NIST Cybersecurity Framework Version 1.1				Sector-Specific Standards and Best Practices		
Function	Category	Subcategory	NIST SP 800-53 Revision 4	IEC TR 80001-2-2	HIPAA Security Rule	ISO/IEC 27001
		DE.CM-6: External service provider activity is monitored to detect potential cybersecurity events.	CA-7, PS-7, SA-4, SA-9, SI-4	RDMP	45 C.F.R. § 164.308(a)(1)(ii)(D)	A.14.2.7, A.15.2.1
		DE.CM-7: Monitoring for unauthorized personnel, connections, devices, and software is performed.	AU-12, CA-7, CM-3, CM-8, PE-3, PE-6, PE-20, SI-4	AUDT, CNFS, PAUT, PLOK, MLDP, NAUT, SGUD	45 C.F.R. §§ 164.308(a)(1)(ii)(D), 164.308(a)(5)(ii)(B), 164.308(a)(5)(ii)(C), 164.310(a)(1), 164.310(a)(2)(ii), 164.310(a)(2)(iii), 164.310(b), 164.310(c), 164.310(d)(1), 164.310(d)(2)(iii), 164.312(b), 164.314(b)(2)(i)	None
		DE.CM-8: Vulnerability scans are performed.	RA-5	MLDP	45 C.F.R. §§ 164.308(a)(1)(i), 164.308(a)(8)	A.12.6.1
RESPOND (RS)	Response Planning (RS.RP)	RS.RP-1: Response plan is executed during or after an event.	CP-2, CP-10, IR-4, IR-8	DTBK, SGUD, MLDP	45 C.F.R. §§ 164.308(a)(6)(ii), 164.308(a)(7)(i), 164.308(a)(7)(ii)(A), 164.308(a)(7)(ii)(B), 164.308(a)(7)(ii)(C), 164.310(a)(2)(i), 164.312(a)(2)(ii)	A.16.1.5

NIST Cybersecurity Framework Version 1.1			Sector-Specific Standards and Best Practices			
Function	Category	Subcategory	NIST SP 800-53 Revision 4	IEC TR 80001-2-2	HIPAA Security Rule	ISO/IEC 27001
	Improvements (RS.IM)	RS.IM-1: Response plans incorporate lessons learned.	CP-2, IR-4, IR-8	DTBK	45 C.F.R. §§ 164.308(a)(7)(ii)(D), 164.308(a)(8), 164.316(b)(2)(iii)	A.16.1.6
		RS.IM-2: Response strategies are updated.	CP-2, IR-4, IR-8	DTBK	45 C.F.R. §§ 164.308(a)(7)(ii)(D), 164.308(a)(8)	None
RECOVER (RC)	Recovery Planning (RC.RP)	RC.RP-1: Recovery plan is executed during or after an event.	CP-10, IR-4, IR-8	DTBK	45 C.F.R. §§ 164.308(a)(7), 164.310(a)(2)(i)	A.16.1.5

APPENDIX A REFERENCES

[1]   Foley & Lardner LLP, "2017 Telemedicine and Digital Health Survey: Telemedicine Surges
        Ahead as Providers, Patients Embrace Technology," 2017.
        Available: https://www.foley.com/files/uploads/2017-Telemedicine-Survey-Report-11-
        8-17.pdf.

[2]   Maryland Health Care Commission, "Remote Patient Monitoring Telehealth Grants: Brief
        and Final Reports," Mar. 2017.
        Available: http://mhcc.maryland.gov/mhcc/pages/hit/hit_telemedicine/documents/Tele
        health_Brief_Reports_FINAL_031617.pdf.

[3]   G. O'Brien et al., *Securing Electronic Health Records on Mobile Devices,* National
        Institute of Standards and Technology (NIST) Special Publication (SP) 1800-1,
        Gaithersburg, Md., Jul. 2018.
        Available: https://www.nccoe.nist.gov/sites/default/files/library/sp1800/hit-ehr-nist-
        sp1800-1.pdf.

[4]   G. O'Brien et al., *Securing Wireless Infusion Pumps in Healthcare Delivery Organizations,*
        NIST SP 1800-8, Gaithersburg, Md., Aug. 2018.
        Available: https://www.nccoe.nist.gov/sites/default/files/library/sp1800/hit-wip-nist-
        sp1800-8.pdf.

AAMI	Association for Advancement of Medical Instrumentation
API	Application Programming Interface
BMI	Body Mass Index
DE	Detect
FDA	Food and Drug Administration
FIPS	Federal Information Processing Standard
GRC	Governance, Risk, and Compliance
HDO	Health Delivery Organization
HHS	Department of Health and Human Services
HIPAA	Health Insurance Portability and Accountability Act
ID	Identify
IdAM	Identity and Access Management
IDS	Intrusion Detection System
IEC	International Electrotechnical Commission
IPS	Intrusion Prevention System
ISO	International Organization for Standardization
IT	Information Technology
NCCoE	National Cybersecurity Center of Excellence
NIST	National Institute of Standards and Technology
PAM	Privileged Access Management
PR	Protect
RC	Recover
RPM	Remote Patient Monitoring
RS	Respond
SDK	Software Development Kit
SP	Special Publication
TR	Technical Report
VPN	Virtual Private Network

HIPAA Security Rule Crosswalk to NIST Cybersecurity Framework

In February 2014, NIST released the Framework for Improving Critical Infrastructure Cybersecurity (Cybersecurity Framework) as directed in Executive Order 13636, Improving Critical Infrastructure Cybersecurity. The Cybersecurity Framework provides a voluntary, risk-based approach—based on existing standards, guidelines, and practices—to help organizations in any industry to understand, communicate, and manage cybersecurity risks. In the health care space, entities (covered entities and business associates) regulated by the Health Insurance Portability and Accountability Act (HIPAA) must comply with the HIPAA Security Rule to ensure the confidentiality, integrity, and availability of electronic protected health information (ePHI) that they create, receive, maintain, or transmit. This crosswalk document identifies "mappings" between the Cybersecurity Framework and the HIPAA Security Rule.

Organizations that have already aligned their security programs to either the NIST Cybersecurity Framework or the HIPAA Security Rule may find this crosswalk helpful as a starting place to identify potential gaps in their programs. Addressing these gaps can bolster their compliance with the Security Rule and improve their ability to secure ePHI and other critical information and business processes. For example, if a covered entity has an existing security program aligned to the HIPAA Security Rule, the entity can use this mapping document to identify which pieces of the NIST Cybersecurity Framework it is already meeting and which represent new practices to incorporate into its risk management program. This mapping document also allows organizations to communicate activities and outcomes internally and externally regarding their cybersecurity program by utilizing the Cybersecurity Framework as a common language. Finally, the mapping can be easily combined with similar mappings to account for additional organizational considerations (e.g., privacy, regulation and legislation). Additional resources, including a FAQ and overview, are available to assist organizations with the use and implementation of the NIST Cybersecurity Framework.

This crosswalk maps each administrative, physical and technical safeguard standard and implementation specification[1] in the HIPAA Security Rule to a relevant NIST Cybersecurity Framework Subcategory. Due to the granularity of the NIST Cybersecurity

---

[1] Although all Security Rule administrative, physical, and technical safeguards map to at least one of the NIST Cybersecurity Framework Subcategories, other Security Rule standards, such as specific requirements for documentation and organization, do not. HIPAA covered entities and business associates cannot rely entirely on the crosswalk for compliance with the Security Rule.

Framework's Subcategories, some HIPAA Security Rule requirements may map to more than one Subcategory. Activities to be performed for a particular Subcategory of the NIST Cybersecurity Framework may be more specific and detailed than those performed for the mapped HIPAA Security Rule requirement. However, the HIPAA Security Rule is designed to be flexible, scalable and technology-neutral, which enables it to accommodate integration with frameworks such as the NIST Cybersecurity Framework. A HIPAA covered entity or business associate should be able to assess and implement new and evolving technologies and best practices that it determines would be reasonable and appropriate to ensure the confidentiality, integrity and availability of the ePHI it creates, receives, maintains, or transmits.

The mappings between the Framework subcategories and the HIPAA Security Rule are intended to be an informative reference and do not imply or guarantee compliance with any laws or regulations. Users who have aligned their security program to the NIST Cybersecurity Framework should not assume that by so doing they are in full compliance with the Security Rule. Conversely, the HIPAA Security Rule does not require covered entities to integrate the Cybersecurity Framework into their security management programs. Covered entities and business associates should perform their own security risk analyses to identify and mitigate threats to the ePHI they create, receive, maintain or transmit. Whether starting a new security program or reviewing an existing one, organizations will want to visit OCR's Security Rule compliance guidance; HealthIT.gov for resources on cybersecurity, security risk assessments, security training; as well as the FDA's guidance on cybersecurity for medical devices. To find assistance with the use and implementation of the NIST Cybersecurity Framework, organizations may explore the C-Cubed Voluntary Program and NIST's frequently asked questions.

The table below incorporates mappings of HIPAA Security Rule standards and implementation specifications to applicable NIST Cybersecurity Framework Subcategories. These mappings are included in the "Relevant Control Mappings" column which also includes mappings from other security frameworks. The other columns ("Function", "Category", and "Subcategory") correlate directly to the Function, Category and Subcategory Unique Identifiers defined within the NIST Cybersecurity Framework. Other frameworks included in the mapping to the NIST Cybersecurity Framework include: the Council on Cybersecurity Critical Security Controls (CCS CSC); Control Objectives for Information and Related Technology Edition 5 (COBIT 5); International Organization for Standardization/ International Electrotechnical Commission (ISO/IEC) 27001; International Society of Automation (ISA) 62443; National Institute of Standards and Technology (NIST) SP 800-53 Rev. 4.

February, 2016

Function	Category	Subcategory	Relevant Control Mappings[2]
	Asset Management (ID.AM): The data, personnel, devices, systems, and facilities that enable the organization to achieve business purposes are identified and managed consistent with their relative importance to business objectives and the organization's risk strategy.	**ID.AM-1:** Physical devices and systems within the organization are inventoried	• CCS CSC 1 • COBIT 5 BAI09.01, BAI09.02 • ISA 62443-2-1:2009 4.2.3.4 • ISA 62443-3-3:2013 SR 7.8 • ISO/IEC 27001:2013 A.8.1.1, A.8.1.2 • NIST SP 800-53 Rev. 4 CM-8 • HIPAA Security Rule 45 C.F.R. §§ 164.308(a)(1)(ii)(A), 164.310(a)(2)(ii), 164.310(d)
		ID.AM-2: Software platforms and applications within the organization are inventoried	• CCS CSC 2 • COBIT 5 BAI09.01, BAI09.02, BAI09.05 • ISA 62443-2-1:2009 4.2.3.4 • ISA 62443-3-3:2013 SR 7.8 • ISO/IEC 27001:2013 A.8.1.1, A.8.1.2 • NIST SP 800-53 Rev. 4 CM-8 • HIPAA Security Rule 45 C.F.R. §§ 164.308(a)(1)(ii)(A), 164.308(a)(7)(ii)(E)
		ID.AM-3: Organizational communication and data flows are mapped	• CCS CSC 1 • COBIT 5 DSS05.02 • ISA 62443-2-1:2009 4.2.3.4 • ISO/IEC 27001:2013 A.13.2.1 • NIST SP 800-53 Rev. 4 AC-4, CA-3, CA-9, PL-8 • HIPAA Security Rule 45 C.F.R. §§ 164.308(a)(1)(ii)(A), 164.308(a)(3)(ii)(A), 164.308(a)(8), 164.310(d)

[2] Mappings to other standards come from the NIST Cybersecurity Framework, Appendix A and are provided for reference

DHHS Office for Civil Rights | *HIPAA Security Rule Crosswalk to NIST Cybersecurity Framework*

Function	Category	Subcategory	Relevant Control Mappings[2]
		ID.AM-4: External information systems are catalogued	• COBIT 5 APO02.02 • ISO/IEC 27001:2013 A.11.2.6 • NIST SP 800-53 Rev. 4 AC-20, SA-9 • HIPAA Security Rule 45 C.F.R. §§ 164.308(a)(4)(ii)(A), 164.308(b), 164.314(a)(1), 164.314(a)(2)(i)(B), 164.314(a)(2)(ii), 164.316(b)(2)
		ID.AM-5: Resources (e.g., hardware, devices, data, and software) are prioritized based on their classification, criticality, and business value	• COBIT 5 APO03.03, APO03.04, BAI09.02 • ISA 62443-2-1:2009 4.2.3.6 • ISO/IEC 27001:2013 A.8.2.1 • NIST SP 800-53 Rev. 4 CP-2, RA-2, SA-14 • HIPAA Security Rule 45 C.F.R. § 164.308(a)(7)(ii)(E)
		ID.AM-6: Cybersecurity roles and responsibilities for the entire workforce and third-party stakeholders (e.g, suppliers, customers, partners) are established	• COBIT 5 APO01.02, DSS06.03 • ISA 62443-2-1:2009 4.3.2.3.3 • ISO/IEC 27001:2013 A.6.1.1 • NIST SP 800-53 Rev. 4 CP-2, PS-7, PM-11 • HIPAA Security Rule 45 C.F.R. §§ 164.308(a)(2), 164.308(a)(3), 164.308(a)(4), 164.308(b)(1), 164.314

Function	Category	Subcategory	Relevant Control Mappings[2]
	Business Environment (ID.BE): The organization's mission, objectives, stakeholders, and activities are understood and prioritized; this information is used to inform cybersecurity roles, responsibilities, and risk management decisions.	**ID.BE-1:** The organization's role in the supply chain is identified and communicated	• COBIT 5 APO08.04, APO08.05, APO10.03, APO10.04, APO10.05 • ISO/IEC 27001:2013 A.15.1.3, A.15.2.1, A.15.2.2 • NIST SP 800-53 Rev. 4 CP-2, SA-12 • HIPAA Security Rule 45 C.F.R. §§ 164.308(a)(1)(ii)(A), 164.308(a)(4)(ii), 164.308(a)(7)(ii)(C), 164.308(a)(7)(ii)(E), 164.308(a)(8), 164.310(a)(2)(i), 164.314, 164.316
		ID.BE-2: The organization's place in critical infrastructure and its industry sector is identified and communicated	• COBIT 5 APO02.06, APO03.01 • NIST SP 800-53 Rev. 4 PM-8 • HIPAA Security Rule 45 C.F.R. §§ 164.308(a)(1)(ii)(A), 164.308(a)(4)(ii), 164.308(a)(7)(ii)(C), 164.308(a)(7)(ii)(E), 164.308(a)(8), 164.310(a)(2)(i), 164.314, 164.316
		ID.BE-3: Priorities for organizational mission, objectives, and activities are established and communicated	• COBIT 5 APO02.01, APO02.06, APO03.01 • ISA 62443-2-1:2009 4.2.2.1, 4.2.3.6 • NIST SP 800-53 Rev. 4 PM-11, SA-14 • HIPAA Security Rule 45 C.F.R. §§ 164.308(a)(7)(ii)(B), 164.308(a)(7)(ii)(C), 164.308(a)(7)(ii)(D), 164.308(a)(7)(ii)(E), 164.310(a)(2)(i), 164.316

Function	Category	Subcategory	Relevant Control Mappings[2]
		ID.BE-4: Dependencies and critical functions for delivery of critical services are established	• ISO/IEC 27001:2013 A.11.2.2, A.11.2.3, A.12.1.3 • NIST SP 800-53 Rev. 4 CP-8, PE-9, PE-11, PM-8, SA-14 • HIPAA Security Rule 45 C.F.R. §§ 164.308(a)(7)(i), 164.308.(a)(7)(ii)(E), 164.310(a)(2)(i), 164.312(a)(2)(ii), 164.314(a)(1), 164.314(b)(2)(i)
		ID.BE-5: Resilience requirements to support delivery of critical services are established	• COBIT 5 DSS04.02 • ISO/IEC 27001:2013 A.11.1.4, A.17.1.1, A.17.1.2, A.17.2.1 • NIST SP 800-53 Rev. 4 CP-2, CP-11, SA-14 • HIPAA Security Rule 45 C.F.R. §§ 164.308(a)(1)(ii)(B), 164.308(a)(6)(ii), 164.308(a)(7), 164.308(a)(8), 164.310(a)(2)(i), 164.312(a)(2)(ii), 164.314(b)(2)(i)
IDENTIFY (ID)	**Governance (ID.GV):** The policies, procedures, and processes to manage and monitor the organization's regulatory, legal, risk, environmental, and operational requirements are understood and inform the management of cybersecurity risk.	**ID.GV-1:** Organizational information security policy is established	• COBIT 5 APO13.12 • ISA 62443-2-1:2009 4.3.2.3.3 • ISO/IEC 27001:2013 A.6.1.1, A.7.2.1 • NIST SP 800-53 Rev. 4 PM-1, PS-7 • HIPAA Security Rule 45 C.F.R. §§ 164.308(a)(1)(i), 164.316
		ID.GV-2: Information security roles & responsibilities are coordinated and aligned with internal roles and external partners	• COBIT 5 APO13.12 • ISA 62443-2-1:2009 4.3.2.3.3 • ISO/IEC 27001:2013 A.6.1.1, A.7.2.1 • NIST SP 800-53 Rev. 4 PM-1, PS-7 • HIPAA Security Rule 45 C.F.R. §§ 164.308(a)(1)(i), 164.308(a)(2), 164.308(a)(3), 164.308(a)(4), 164.308(b), 164.314

Function	Category	Subcategory	Relevant Control Mappings[2]
		ID.GV-3: Legal and regulatory requirements regarding cybersecurity, including privacy and civil liberties obligations, are understood and managed	• COBIT 5 MEA03.01, MEA03.04 • ISA 62443-2-1:2009 4.4.3.7 • ISO/IEC 27001:2013 A.18.1 • NIST SP 800-53 Rev. 4 -1 controls from all families (except PM-1) • HIPAA Security Rule 45 C.F.R. §§ 164.306, 164.308, 164.310, 164.312, 164.314, 164.316
		ID.GV-4: Governance and risk management processes address cybersecurity risks	• COBIT 5 DSS04.02 • ISA 62443-2-1:2009 4.2.3.1, 4.2.3.3, 4.2.3.8, 4.2.3.9, 4.2.3.11, 4.3.2.4.3, 4.3.2.6.3 • NIST SP 800-53 Rev. 4 PM-9, PM-11 • HIPAA Security Rule 45 C.F.R. §§ 164.308(a)(1), 164.308(b)
	Risk Assessment (ID.RA): The organization understands the cybersecurity risk to organizational operations (including mission, functions, image, or reputation), organizational assets, and individuals.	**ID.RA-1:** Asset vulnerabilities are identified and documented	• CCS CSC 4 • COBIT 5 APO12.01, APO12.02, APO12.03, APO12.04 • ISA 62443-2-1:2009 4.2.3, 4.2.3.7, 4.2.3.9, 4.2.3.12 • ISO/IEC 27001:2013 A.12.6.1, A.18.2.3 • NIST SP 800-53 Rev. 4 CA-2, CA-7, CA-8, RA-3, RA-5, SA-5, SA-11, SI-2, SI-4, SI-5 • HIPAA Security Rule 45 C.F.R. §§ 164.308(a)(1)(ii)(A), 164.308(a)(7)(ii)(E), 164.308(a)(8), 164.310(a)(1), 164.312(a)(1), 164.316(b)(2)(iii)

Function	Category	Subcategory	Relevant Control Mappings[2]
		ID.RA-2: Threat and vulnerability information is received from information sharing forums and sources	• ISA 62443-2-1:2009 4.2.3, 4.2.3.9, 4.2.3.12 • ISO/IEC 27001:2013 A.6.1.4 • NIST SP 800-53 Rev. 4 PM-15, PM-16, SI-5 • No direct analog to HIPAA Security Rule[3]
		ID.RA-3: Threats, both internal and external, are identified and documented	• COBIT 5 APO12.01, APO12.02, APO12.03, APO12.04 • ISA 62443-2-1:2009 4.2.3, 4.2.3.9, 4.2.3.12 • NIST SP 800-53 Rev. 4 RA-3, SI-5, PM-12, PM-16 • HIPAA Security Rule 45 C.F.R. §§ 164.308(a)(1)(ii)(A), 164.308(a)(1)(ii)(D), 164.308(a)(3), 164.308(a)(4), 164.308(a)(5)(ii)(A), 164.310(a)(1), 164.310(a)(2)(iii), 164.312(a)(1), 164.312(c), 164.312(e), 164.314, 164.316
		ID.RA-4: Potential business impacts and likelihoods are identified	• COBIT 5 DSS04.02 • ISA 62443-2-1:2009 4.2.3, 4.2.3.9, 4.2.3.12 • NIST SP 800-53 Rev. 4 RA-2, RA-3, PM-9, PM-11, SA-14 • HIPAA Security Rule 45 C.F.R. §§ 164.308(a)(1)(i), 164.308(a)(1)(ii)(A), 164.308(a)(1)(ii)(B), 164.308(a)(6), 164.308(a)(7)(ii)(E), 164.308(a)(8), 164.316(a)

[3] Even though there is no direct analog, while performing their HIPAA Security Rule required risk analysis, organizations should consider whether participating in cyber-threat sharing programs is reasonable and appropriate to reduce their security risk.

Function	Category	Subcategory	Relevant Control Mappings[2]
		ID.RA-5: Threats, vulnerabilities, likelihoods, and impacts are used to determine risk	• COBIT 5 APO12.02 • ISO/IEC 27001:2013 A.12.6.1 • NIST SP 800-53 Rev. 4 RA-2, RA-3, PM-16 • HIPAA Security Rule 45 C.F.R. §§ 164.308(a)(1)(ii)(A), 164.308(a)(1)(ii)(B), 164.308(a)(1)(ii)(D), 164.308(a)(7)(ii)(D), 164.308(a)(7)(ii)(E), 164.316(a)
		ID.RA-6: Risk responses are identified and prioritized	• COBIT 5 APO12.05, APO13.02 • NIST SP 800-53 Rev. 4 PM-4, PM-9 • HIPAA Security Rule 45 C.F.R. §§ 164.308(a)(1)(ii)(B), 164.314(a)(2)(i)(C), 164.314(b)(2)(iv)
	Risk Management Strategy (ID.RM): The organization's priorities, constraints, risk tolerances, and assumptions are established and used to support operational risk decisions.	**ID.RM-1:** Risk management processes are established, managed, and agreed to by organizational stakeholders	• COBIT 5 APO12.04, APO12.05, APO13.02, BAI02.03, BAI04.02 • ISA 62443-2-1:2009 4.3.4.2 • NIST SP 800-53 Rev. 4 PM-9 • HIPAA Security Rule 45 C.F.R. § 164.308(a)(1)(ii)(B)
		ID.RM-2: Organizational risk tolerance is determined and clearly expressed	• COBIT 5 APO12.06 • ISA 62443-2-1:2009 4.3.2.6.5 • NIST SP 800-53 Rev. 4 PM-9 • HIPAA Security Rule 45 C.F.R. § 164.308(a)(1)(ii)(B)

Function	Category	Subcategory	Relevant Control Mappings[2]
		ID.RM-3: The organization's determination of risk tolerance is informed by its role in critical infrastructure and sector specific risk analysis	• NIST SP 800-53 Rev. 4 PM-8, PM-9, PM-11, SA-14 • HIPAA Security Rule 45 C.F.R. §§ 164.308(a)(1)(ii)(B), 164.308(a)(6)(ii), 164.308(a)(7)(i), 164.308(a)(7)(ii)(C),164.308(a)(7)(ii)(E), 164.310(a)(2)(i)
	Access Control (PR.AC): Access to assets and associated facilities is limited to authorized users, processes, or devices, and to authorized activities and transactions.	**PR.AC-1:** Identities and credentials are managed for authorized devices and users	• CCS CSC 16 • COBIT 5 DSS05.04, DSS06.03 • ISA 62443-2-1:2009 4.3.3.5.1 • ISA 62443-3-3:2013 SR 1.1, SR 1.2, SR 1.3, SR 1.4, SR 1.5, SR 1.7, SR 1.8, SR 1.9 • ISO/IEC 27001:2013 A.9.2.1, A.9.2.2, A.9.2.4, A.9.3.1, A.9.4.2, A.9.4.3 • NIST SP 800-53 Rev. 4 AC-2, IA Family • HIPAA Security Rule 45 C.F.R. §§ 164.308(a)(3)(ii)(B), 164.308(a)(3)(ii)(C), 164.308(a)(4)(i), 164.308(a)(4)(ii)(B), 164.308(a)(4)(ii)(C), 164.312(a)(2)(i), 164.312(a)(2)(ii), 164.312(a)(2)(iii), 164.312(d)

Function	Category	Subcategory	Relevant Control Mappings[2]
		PR.AC-2: Physical access to assets is managed and protected	• COBIT 5 DSS01.04, DSS05.05 • ISA 62443-2-1:2009 4.3.3.3.2, 4.3.3.3.8 • ISO/IEC 27001:2013 A.11.1.1, A.11.1.2, A.11.1.4, A.11.1.6, A.11.2.3 • NIST SP 800-53 Rev. 4 PE-2, PE-3, PE-4, PE-5, PE-6, PE-9 • HIPAA Security Rule 45 C.F.R. §§ 164.308(a)(1)(ii)(B), 164.308(a)(7)(i), 164.308(a)(7)(ii)(A), 164.310(a)(1), 164.310(a)(2)(i), 164.310(a)(2)(ii), 164.310(a)(2)(iii), 164.310(b), 164.310(c), 164.310(d)(1), 164.310(d)(2)(iii)
		PR.AC-3: Remote access is managed	• COBIT 5 APO13.01, DSS01.04, DSS05.03 • ISA 62443-2-1:2009 4.3.3.6.6 • ISA 62443-3-3:2013 SR 1.13, SR 2.6 • ISO/IEC 27001:2013 A.6.2.2, A.13.1.1, A.13.2.1 • NIST SP 800-53 Rev. 4 AC-17, AC-19, AC-20 • HIPAA Security Rule 45 C.F.R. §§ 164.308(a)(4)(i), 164.308(b)(1), 164.308(b)(3), 164.310(b), 164.312(e)(1), 164.312(e)(2)(ii)

Function	Category	Subcategory	Relevant Control Mappings[2]
		PR.AC-4: Access permissions are managed, incorporating the principles of least privilege and separation of duties	• CCS CSC 12, 15 • ISA 62443-2-1:2009 4.3.3.7.3 • ISA 62443-3-3:2013 SR 2.1 • ISO/IEC 27001:2013 A.6.1.2, A.9.1.2, A.9.2.3, A.9.4.1, A.9.4.4 • NIST SP 800-53 Rev. 4 AC-2, AC-3, AC-5, AC-6, AC-16 • HIPAA Security Rule 45 C.F.R. §§ 164.308(a)(3), 164.308(a)(4), 164.310(a)(2)(iii), 164.310(b), 164.312(a)(1), 164.312(a)(2)(i), 164.312(a)(2)(ii)
		PR.AC-5: Network integrity is protected, incorporating network segregation where appropriate	• ISA 62443-2-1:2009 4.3.3.4 • ISA 62443-3-3:2013 SR 3.1, SR 3.8 • ISO/IEC 27001:2013 A.13.1.1, A.13.1.3, A.13.2.1 • NIST SP 800-53 Rev. 4 AC-4, SC-7 • HIPAA Security Rule 45 C.F.R. §§ 164.308(a)(4)(ii)(B), 164.310(a)(1), 164.310(b), 164.312(a)(1), 164.312(b), 164.312(c), 164.312(e)

Function	Category	Subcategory	Relevant Control Mappings[2]
	Awareness and Training (PR.AT): The organization's personnel and partners are provided cybersecurity awareness education and are adequately trained to perform their information security-related duties and responsibilities consistent with related policies, procedures, and agreements.	**PR.AT-1:** All users are informed and trained	• CCS CSC 9 • COBIT 5 APO07.03, BAI05.07 • ISA 62443-2-1:2009 4.3.2.4.2 • ISO/IEC 27001:2013 A.7.2.2 • NIST SP 800-53 Rev. 4 AT-2, PM-13 • HIPAA Security Rule 45 C.F.R. § 164.308(a)(5)
		PR.AT-2: Privileged users understand roles & responsibilities	• CCS CSC 9 • COBIT 5 APO07.02, DSS06.03 • ISA 62443-2-1:2009 4.3.2.4.2, 4.3.2.4.3 • ISO/IEC 27001:2013 A.6.1.1, A.7.2.2 • NIST SP 800-53 Rev. 4 AT-3, PM-13 • HIPAA Security Rule 45 C.F.R. §§ 164.308(a)(2), 164.308(a)(3)(i), 164.308(a)(5)(i), 164.308(a)(5)(ii)(A), 164.308(a)(5)(ii)(B), 164.308(a)(5)(ii)(C), 164.308(a)(5)(ii)(D)
		PR.AT-3: Third-party stakeholders (e.g., suppliers, customers, partners) understand roles & responsibilities	• CCS CSC 9 • COBIT 5 APO07.03, APO10.04, APO10.05 • ISA 62443-2-1:2009 4.3.2.4.2 • ISO/IEC 27001:2013 A.6.1.1, A.7.2.2 • NIST SP 800-53 Rev. 4 PS-7, SA-9 • HIPAA Security Rule 45 C.F.R. §§ 164.308(b), 164.314(a)(1), 164.314(a)(2)(i), 164.314(a)(2)(ii)

Function	Category	Subcategory	Relevant Control Mappings[2]
		PR.AT-4: Senior executives understand roles & responsibilities	• CCS CSC 9 • COBIT 5 APO07.03 • ISA 62443-2-1:2009 4.3.2.4.2 • ISO/IEC 27001:2013 A.6.1.1, A.7.2.2, • NIST SP 800-53 Rev. 4 AT-3, PM-13 • HIPAA Security Rule 45 C.F.R. §§ 164.308(a)(2), 164.308(a)(3)(i), 164.308(a)(5)(i), 164.308(a)(5)(ii)(A), 164.308(a)(5)(ii)(B), 164.308(a)(5)(ii)(C), 164.308(a)(5)(ii)(D)
		PR.AT-5: Physical and information security personnel understand roles & responsibilities	• CCS CSC 9 • COBIT 5 APO07.03 • ISA 62443-2-1:2009 4.3.2.4.2 • ISO/IEC 27001:2013 A.6.1.1, A.7.2.2, • NIST SP 800-53 Rev. 4 AT-3, PM-13 • HIPAA Security Rule 45 C.F.R. §§ 164.308(a)(2), 164.308(a)(3)(i), 164.308(a)(5)(i), 164.308(a)(5)(ii)(A), 164.308(a)(5)(ii)(B), 164.308(a)(5)(ii)(C), 164.308(a)(5)(ii)(D), 164.530(b)(1)
	Data Security (PR.DS): Information and records (data) are managed consistent with the organization's risk strategy to protect the confidentiality, integrity, and availability of information.	**PR.DS-1:** Data-at-rest is protected	• CCS CSC 17 • COBIT 5 APO01.06, BAI02.01, BAI06.01, DSS06.06 • ISA 62443-3-3:2013 SR 3.4, SR 4.1 • ISO/IEC 27001:2013 A.8.2.3 • NIST SP 800-53 Rev. 4 SC-28 • HIPAA Security Rule 45 C.F.R. §§ 164.308(a)(1)(ii)(D), 164.308(b)(1), 164.310(d), 164.312(a)(1), 164.312(a)(2)(iii), 164.312(a)(2)(iv), 164.312(b), 164.312(c), 164.314(b)(2)(i), 164.312(d)

Function	Category	Subcategory	Relevant Control Mappings[2]
		PR.DS-2: Data-in-transit is protected	• CCS CSC 17 • COBIT 5 APO01.06, DSS06.06 • ISA 62443-3-3:2013 SR 3.1, SR 3.8, SR 4.1, SR 4.2 • ISO/IEC 27001:2013 A.8.2.3, A.13.1.1, A.13.2.1, A.13.2.3, A.14.1.2, A.14.1.3 • NIST SP 800-53 Rev. 4 SC-8 • HIPAA Security Rule 45 C.F.R. §§ 164.308(b)(1), 164.308(b)(2), 164.312(e)(1), 164.312(e)(2)(i), 164.312(e)(2)(ii), 164.314(b)(2)(i)
		PR.DS-3: Assets are formally managed throughout removal, transfers, and disposition	• COBIT 5 BAI09.03 • ISA 62443-2-1:2009 4. 4.3.3.3.9, 4.3.4.4.1 • ISA 62443-3-3:2013 SR 4.2 • ISO/IEC 27001:2013 A.8.2.3, A.8.3.1, A.8.3.2, A.8.3.3, A.11.2.7 • NIST SP 800-53 Rev. 4 CM-8, MP-6, PE-16 • HIPAA Security Rule 45 C.F.R. §§ 164.308(a)(1)(ii)(A), 164.310(a)(2)(ii), 164.310(a)(2)(iii), 164.310(a)(2)(iv), 164.310(d)(1), 164.310(d)(2)
		PR.DS-4: Adequate capacity to ensure availability is maintained	• COBIT 5 APO13.01 • ISA 62443-3-3:2013 SR 7.1, SR 7.2 • ISO/IEC 27001:2013 A.12.3.1 • NIST SP 800-53 Rev. 4 AU-4, CP-2, SC-5 • HIPAA Security Rule 45 C.F.R. §§ 164.308(a)(1)(ii)(A), 164.308(a)(1)(ii)(B), 164.308(a)(7), 164.310(a)(2)(i), 164.310(d)(2)(iv), 164.312(a)(2)(ii)

Function	Category	Subcategory	Relevant Control Mappings[2]
		PR.DS-5: Protections against data leaks are implemented	• CCS CSC 17 • COBIT 5 APO01.06 • ISA 62443-3-3:2013 SR 5.2 • ISO/IEC 27001:2013 A.6.1.2, A.7.1.1, A.7.1.2, A.7.3.1, A.8.2.2, A.8.2.3, A.9.1.1, A.9.1.2, A.9.2.3, A.9.4.1, A.9.4.4, A.9.4.5, A.13.1.3, A.13.2.1, A.13.2.3, A.13.2.4, A.14.1.2, A.14.1.3 • NIST SP 800-53 Rev. 4 AC-4, AC-5, AC-6, PE-19, PS-3, PS-6, SC-7, SC-8, SC-13, SC-31, SI-4 • HIPAA Security Rule 45 C.F.R. §§ 164.308(a)(1)(ii)(D), 164.308(a)(3), 164.308(a)(4), 164.310(b), 164.310(c), 164.312(a), 164.312(e)
		PR.DS-6: Integrity checking mechanisms are used to verify software, firmware, and information integrity	• ISA 62443-3-3:2013 SR 3.1, SR 3.3, SR 3.4, SR 3.8 • ISO/IEC 27001:2013 A.12.2.1, A.12.5.1, A.14.1.2, A.14.1.3 • NIST SP 800-53 Rev. 4 SI-7 • HIPAA Security Rule 45 C.F.R. §§ 164.308(a)(1)(ii)(D), 164.312(b), 164.312(c)(1), 164.312(c)(2), 164.312(e)(2)(i)

Function	Category	Subcategory	Relevant Control Mappings[2]
		PR.DS-7: The development and testing environment(s) are separate from the production environment	• COBIT 5 BAI07.04 • ISO/IEC 27001:2013 A.12.1.4 • NIST SP 800-53 Rev. 4 CM-2 • HIPAA Security Rule 45 C.F.R. § 164.308(a)(4)[4]
PROTECT	**Information Protection Processes and Procedures (PR.IP):** Security policies (that address purpose, scope, roles, responsibilities, management commitment, and coordination among organizational entities), processes, and procedures are maintained and used to manage protection of information systems and assets.	**PR.IP-1:** A baseline configuration of information technology/industrial control systems is created and maintained	• CCS CSC 3, 10 • COBIT 5 BAI10.01, BAI10.02, BAI10.03, BAI10.05 • ISA 62443-2-1:2009 4.3.4.3.2, 4.3.4.3.3 • ISA 62443-3-3:2013 SR 7.6 • ISO/IEC 27001:2013 A.12.1.2, A.12.5.1, A.12.6.2, A.14.2.2, A.14.2.3, A.14.2.4 • NIST SP 800-53 Rev. 4 CM-2, CM-3, CM-4, CM-5, CM-6, CM-7, CM-9, SA-10 • HIPAA Security Rule 45 C.F.R. §§ 164.308(a)(8), 164.308(a)(7)(i), 164.308(a)(7)(ii)

---

[4] Additionally, organizations should consider the HIPAA Privacy Rule "minimum necessary" standard, 45 C.F.R. § 164.502(b), when determining the level of access that is appropriate for development and testing staff.

Function (PR)	Category	Subcategory	Relevant Control Mappings[2]
		PR.IP-2: A System Development Life Cycle to manage systems is implemented	• COBIT 5 APO13.01 • ISA 62443-2-1:2009 4.3.4.3.3 • ISO/IEC 27001:2013 A.6.1.5, A.14.1.1, A.14.2.1, A.14.2.5 • NIST SP 800-53 Rev. 4 SA-3, SA-4, SA-8, SA-10, SA-11, SA-12, SA-15, SA-17, PL-8 • HIPAA Security Rule 45 C.F.R. § 164.308(a)(1)(i)
		PR.IP-3: Configuration change control processes are in place	• COBIT 5 BAI06.01, BAI01.06 • ISA 62443-2-1:2009 4.3.4.3.2, 4.3.4.3.3 • ISA 62443-3-3:2013 SR 7.6 • ISO/IEC 27001:2013 A.12.1.2, A.12.5.1, A.12.6.2, A.14.2.2, A.14.2.3, A.14.2.4 • NIST SP 800-53 Rev. 4 CM-3, CM-4, SA-10 • HIPAA Security Rule 45 C.F.R. § 164.308(a)(8)
		PR.IP-4: Backups of information are conducted, maintained, and tested periodically	• COBIT 5 APO13.01 • ISA 62443-2-1:2009 4.3.4.3.9 • ISA 62443-3-3:2013 SR 7.3, SR 7.4 • ISO/IEC 27001:2013 A.12.3.1, A.17.1.2A.17.1.3, A.18.1.3 • NIST SP 800-53 Rev. 4 CP-4, CP-6, CP-9 • HIPAA Security Rule 45 C.F.R. §§ 164.308(a)(7)(ii)(A), 164.308(a)(7)(ii)(B), 164.308(a)(7)(ii)(D), 164.310(a)(2)(i), 164.310(d)(2)(iv)

Function	Category	Subcategory	Relevant Control Mappings[2]
		PR.IP-5: Policy and regulations regarding the physical operating environment for organizational assets are met	• COBIT 5 DSS01.04, DSS05.05 • ISA 62443-2-1:2009 4.3.3.3.1 4.3.3.3.2, 4.3.3.3, 4.3.3.3.5, 4.3.3.3.6 • ISO/IEC 27001:2013 A.11.1.4, A.11.2.1, A.11.2.2, A.11.2.3 • NIST SP 800-53 Rev. 4 PE-10, PE-12, PE-13, PE-14, PE-15, PE-18 • HIPAA Security Rule 45 C.F.R. §§ 164.308(a)(7)(i), 164.308(a)(7)(ii)(C), 164.310, 164.316(b)(2)(iii)
		PR.IP-6: Data is destroyed according to policy	• COBIT 5 BAI09.03 • ISA 62443-2-1:2009 4.3.4.4.4 • ISA 62443-3-3:2013 SR 4.2 • ISO/IEC 27001:2013 A.8.2.3, A.8.3.1, A.8.3.2, A.11.2.7 • NIST SP 800-53 Rev. 4 MP-6 • HIPAA Security Rule 45 C.F.R. §§ 164.310(d)(2)(i), 164.310(d)(2)(ii)
		PR.IP-7: Protection processes are continuously improved	• COBIT 5 APO11.06, DSS04.05 • ISA 62443-2-1:2009 4.4.3.1, 4.4.3.2, 4.4.3.3, 4.4.3.4, 4.4.3.5, 4.4.3.6, 4.4.3.7, 4.4.3.8 • NIST SP 800-53 Rev. 4 CA-2, CA-7, CP-2, IR-8, PL-2, PM-6 • HIPAA Security Rule 45 C.F.R. §§ 164.306(e), 164.308(a)(7)(ii)(D), 164.308(a)(8), 164.316(b)(2)(iii)

Function	Category	Subcategory	Relevant Control Mappings[2]
		PR.IP-8: Effectiveness of protection technologies is shared with appropriate parties	• ISO/IEC 27001:2013 A.16.1.6 • NIST SP 800-53 Rev. 4 AC-21, CA-7, SI-4 • HIPAA Security Rule 45 C.F.R. § 164.308(a)(6)(ii)
		PR.IP-9: Response plans (Incident Response and Business Continuity) and recovery plans (Incident Recovery and Disaster Recovery) are in place and managed	• COBIT 5 DSS04.03 • ISA 62443-2-1:2009 4.3.2.5.3, 4.3.4.5.1 • ISO/IEC 27001:2013 A.16.1.1, A.17.1.1, A.17.1.2 • NIST SP 800-53 Rev. 4 CP-2, IR-8 • HIPAA Security Rule 45 C.F.R. §§ 164.308(a)(6), 164.308(a)(7), 164.310(a)(2)(i), 164.312(a)(2)(ii)
		PR.IP-10: Response and recovery plans are tested	• ISA 62443-2-1:2009 4.3.2.5.7, 4.3.4.5.11 • ISA 62443-3-3:2013 SR 3.3 • ISO/IEC 27001:2013 A.17.1.3 • NIST SP 800-53 Rev.4 CP-4, IR-3, PM-14 • HIPAA Security Rule 45 C.F.R. § 164.308(a)(7)(ii)(D)
		PR.IP-11: Cybersecurity is included in human resources practices (e.g., deprovisioning, personnel screening)	• COBIT 5 APO07.01, APO07.02, APO07.03, APO07.04, APO07.05 • ISA 62443-2-1:2009 4.3.3.2.1, 4.3.3.2.2, 4.3.3.2.3 • ISO/IEC 27001:2013 A.7.1.1, A.7.3.1, A.8.1.4 • NIST SP 800-53 Rev. 4 PS Family • HIPAA Security Rule 45 C.F.R. §§ 164.308(a)(1)(ii)(C), 164.308(a)(3)

Function	Category	Subcategory	Relevant Control Mappings[2]
		PR.IP-12: A vulnerability management plan is developed and implemented	• ISO/IEC 27001:2013 A.12.6.1, A.18.2.2 • NIST SP 800-53 Rev. 4 RA-3, RA-5, SI-2 • HIPAA Security Rule 45 C.F.R. §§ 164.308(a)(1)(i). 164.308(a)(1)(ii)(A), 164.308(a)(1)(ii)(B)
	Maintenance (PR.MA): Maintenance and repairs of industrial control and information system components is performed consistent with policies and procedures.	**PR.MA-1:** Maintenance and repair of organizational assets is performed and logged in a timely manner, with approved and controlled tools	• COBIT 5 BAI09.03 • ISA 62443-2-1:2009 4.3.3.3.7 • ISO/IEC 27001:2013 A.11.1.2, A.11.2.4, A.11.2.5 • NIST SP 800-53 Rev. 4 MA-2, MA-3, MA-5 • HIPAA Security Rule 45 C.F.R. §§ 164.308(a)(3)(ii)(A), 164.310(a)(2)(iv)

Function	Category	Subcategory	Relevant Control Mappings[2]
		PR.MA-2: Remote maintenance of organizational assets is approved, logged, and performed in a manner that prevents unauthorized access	• COBIT 5 DSS05.04 • ISA 62443-2-1:2009 4.3.3.6.5, 4.3.3.6.6, 4.3.3.6.7, 4.4.4.6.8 • ISO/IEC 27001:2013 A.11.2.4, A.15.1.1, A.15.2.1 • NIST SP 800-53 Rev. 4 MA-4 • HIPAA Security Rule 45 C.F.R. §§ 164.308(a)(3)(ii)(A), 164.310(d)(1), 164.310(d)(2)(ii), 164.310(d)(2)(iii), 164.312(a), 164.312(a)(2)(ii), 164.312(a)(2)(iv), 164.312(b), 164.312(d), 164.312(e), 164.308(a)(1)(ii)(D)

Function	Category	Subcategory	Relevant Control Mappings[2]
	Protective Technology (PR.PT): Technical security solutions are managed to ensure the security and resilience of systems and assets, consistent with related policies, procedures, and agreements.	**PR.PT-1:** Audit/log records are determined, documented, implemented, and reviewed in accordance with policy	• CCS CSC 14 • COBIT 5 APO11.04 • ISA 62443-2-1:2009 4.3.3.3.9, 4.3.3.5.8, 4.3.4.4.7, 4.4.2.1, 4.4.2.2, 4.4.2.4 • ISA 62443-3-3:2013 SR 2.8, SR 2.9, SR 2.10, SR 2.11, SR 2.12 • ISO/IEC 27001:2013 A.12.4.1, A.12.4.2, A.12.4.3, A.12.4.4, A.12.7.1 • NIST SP 800-53 Rev. 4 AU Family • HIPAA Security Rule 45 C.F.R. §§ 164.308(a)(1)(ii)(D), 164.308(a)(5)(ii)(C), 164.310(a)(2)(iv), 164.310(d)(2)(iii), 164.312(b)
		PR.PT-2: Removable media is protected and its use restricted according to policy	• COBIT 5 DSS05.02, APO13.01 • ISA 62443-3-3:2013 SR 2.3 • ISO/IEC 27001:2013 A.8.2.2, A.8.2.3, A.8.3.1, A.8.3.3, A.11.2.9 • NIST SP 800-53 Rev. 4 MP-2, MP-4, MP-5, MP-7 • HIPAA Security Rule 45 C.F.R. §§ 164.308(a)(3)(i), 164.308(a)(3)(ii)(A), 164.310(d)(1), 164.310(d)(2), 164.312(a)(1), 164.312(a)(2)(iv), 164.312(b)

Function	Category	Subcategory	Relevant Control Mappings[2]
		PR.PT-3: Access to systems and assets is controlled, incorporating the principle of least functionality	• COBIT 5 DSS05.02 • ISA 62443-2-1:2009 4.3.3.5.1, 4.3.3.5.2, 4.3.3.5.3, 4.3.3.5.4, 4.3.3.5.5, 4.3.3.5.6, 4.3.3.5.7, 4.3.3.5.8, 4.3.3.6.1, 4.3.3.6.2, 4.3.3.6.3, 4.3.3.6.4, 4.3.3.6.5, 4.3.3.6.6, 4.3.3.6.7, 4.3.3.6.8, 4.3.3.6.9, 4.3.3.7.1, 4.3.3.7.2, 4.3.3.7.3, 4.3.3.7.4 • ISA 62443-3-3:2013 SR 1.1, SR 1.2, SR 1.3, SR 1.4, SR 1.5, SR 1.6, SR 1.7, SR 1.8, SR 1.9, SR 1.10, SR 1.11, SR 1.12, SR 1.13, SR 2.1, SR 2.2, SR 2.3, SR 2.4, SR 2.5, SR 2.6, SR 2.7 • ISO/IEC 27001:2013 A.9.1.2 • NIST SP 800-53 Rev. 4 AC-3, CM-7 • HIPAA Security Rule 45 C.F.R. §§ 164.308(a)(3), 164.308(a)(4), 164.310(a)(2)(iii), 164.310(b), 164.310(c), 164.312(a)(1), 164.312(a)(2)(i), 164.312(a)(2)(ii), 164.312(a)(2)(iv)
		PR.PT-4: Communications and control networks are protected	• CCS CSC 7 • COBIT 5 DSS05.02, APO13.01 • ISA 62443-3-3:2013 SR 3.1, SR 3.5, SR 3.8, SR 4.1, SR 4.3, SR 5.1, SR 5.2, SR 5.3, SR 7.1, SR 7.6 • ISO/IEC 27001:2013 A.13.1.1, A.13.2.1 • NIST SP 800-53 Rev. 4 AC-4, AC-17, AC-18, CP-8, SC-7 • HIPAA Security Rule 45 C.F.R. §§ 164.308(a)(1)(ii)(D), 164.312(a)(1), 164.312(b), 164.312(e)

Function	Category	Subcategory	Relevant Control Mappings[2]
	Anomalies and Events (DE.AE): Anomalous activity is detected in a timely manner and the potential impact of events is understood.	**DE.AE-1:** A baseline of network operations and expected data flows for users and systems is established and managed	• COBIT 5 DSS03.01 • ISA 62443-2-1:2009 4.4.3.3 • NIST SP 800-53 Rev. 4 AC-4, CA-3, CM-2, SI-4 • HIPAA Security Rule 45 C.F.R. §§ 164.308(a)(1)(ii)(D), 164.312(b)
		DE.AE-2: Detected events are analyzed to understand attack targets and methods	• ISA 62443-2-1:2009 4.3.4.5.6, 4.3.4.5.7, 4.3.4.5.8 • ISA 62443-3-3:2013 SR 2.8, SR 2.9, SR 2.10, SR 2.11, SR 2.12, SR 3.9, SR 6.1, SR 6.2 • ISO/IEC 27001:2013 A.16.1.1, A.16.1.4 • NIST SP 800-53 Rev. 4 AU-6, CA-7, IR-4, SI-4 • HIPAA Security Rule 45 C.F.R. § 164.308(6)(i)
		DE.AE-3: Event data are aggregated and correlated from multiple sources and sensors	• ISA 62443-3-3:2013 SR 6.1 • NIST SP 800-53 Rev. 4 AU-6, CA-7, IR-4, IR-5, IR-8, SI-4 • HIPAA Security Rule 45 C.F.R. §§ 164.308(a)(1)(ii)(D), 164.308(a)(5)(ii)(B), 164.308(a)(5)(ii)(C), 164.308(a)(6)(ii), 164.308(a)(8), 164.310(d)(2)(iii), 164.312(b), 164.314(a)(2)(i)(C), 164.314(a)(2)(iii)
		DE.AE-4: Impact of events is determined	• COBIT 5 APO12.06 • NIST SP 800-53 Rev. 4 CP-2, IR-4, RA-3, SI-4 • HIPAA Security Rule 45 C.F.R. § 164.308(a)(6)(ii)

Function	Category	Subcategory	Relevant Control Mappings[2]
		DE.AE-5: Incident alert thresholds are established	• COBIT 5 APO12.06 • ISA 62443-2-1:2009 4.2.3.10 • NIST SP 800-53 Rev. 4 IR-4, IR-5, IR-8 • HIPAA Security Rule 45 C.F.R. § 164.308(a)(6)(i)
	Security Continuous Monitoring (DE.CM): The information system and assets are monitored at discrete intervals to identify cybersecurity events and verify the effectiveness of protective measures.	**DE.CM-1:** The network is monitored to detect potential cybersecurity events	• CCS CSC 14, 16 • COBIT 5 DSS05.07 • ISA 62443-3-3:2013 SR 6.2 • NIST SP 800-53 Rev. 4 AC-2, AU-12, CA-7, CM-3, SC-5, SC-7, SI-4 • HIPAA Security Rule 45 C.F.R. §§ 164.308(a)(1)(ii)(D), 164.308(a)(5)(ii)(B), 164.308(a)(5)(ii)(C), 164.308(a)(8), 164.312(b), 164.312(e)(2)(i)
		DE.CM-2: The physical environment is monitored to detect potential cybersecurity events	• ISA 62443-2-1:2009 4.3.3.3.8 • NIST SP 800-53 Rev. 4 CA-7, PE-3, PE-6, PE-20 • HIPAA Security Rule 45 C.F.R. §§ 164.310(a)(2)(ii), 164.310(a)(2)(iii)

Function	Category	Subcategory	Relevant Control Mappings[2]
		DE.CM-3: Personnel activity is monitored to detect potential cybersecurity events	• ISA 62443-3-3:2013 SR 6.2 • ISO/IEC 27001:2013 A.12.4.1 • NIST SP 800-53 Rev. 4 AC-2, AU-12, AU-13, CA-7, CM-10, CM-11 • HIPAA Security Rule 45 C.F.R. §§ 164.308(a)(1)(ii)(D), 164.308(a)(3)(ii)(A), 164.308(a)(5)(ii)(C), 164.312(a)(2)(i), 164.312(b), 164.312(d), 164.312(e)
		DE.CM-4: Malicious code is detected	• CCS CSC 5 • COBIT 5 DSS05.01 • ISA 62443-2-1:2009 4.3.4.3.8 • ISA 62443-3-3:2013 SR 3.2 • ISO/IEC 27001:2013 A.12.2.1 • NIST SP 800-53 Rev. 4 SI-3 • HIPAA Security Rule 45 C.F.R. §§ 164.308(a)(1)(ii)(D), 164.308(a)(5)(ii)(B)
		DE.CM-5: Unauthorized mobile code is detected	• ISA 62443-3-3:2013 SR 2.4 • ISO/IEC 27001:2013 A.12.5.1 • NIST SP 800-53 Rev. 4 SC-18, SI-4. SC-44 • HIPAA Security Rule 45 C.F.R. §§ 164.308(a)(1)(ii)(D), 164.308(a)(5)(ii)(B)
DETECT (DE)		**DE.CM-6:** External service provider activity is monitored to detect potential cybersecurity events	• COBIT 5 APO07.06 • ISO/IEC 27001:2013 A.14.2.7, A.15.2.1 • NIST SP 800-53 Rev. 4 CA-7, PS-7, SA-4, SA-9, SI-4 • HIPAA Security Rule 45 C.F.R. § 164.308(a)(1)(ii)(D)

Function	Category	Subcategory	Relevant Control Mappings[2]
		DE.CM-7: Monitoring for unauthorized personnel, connections, devices, and software is performed	• NIST SP 800-53 Rev. 4 AU-12, CA-7, CM-3, CM-8, PE-3, PE-6, PE-20, SI-4 • HIPAA Security Rule 45 C.F.R. §§ 164.308(a)(1)(ii)(D), 164.308(a)(5)(ii)(B), 164.308(a)(5)(ii)(C), 164.310(a)(1), 164.310(a)(2)(ii), 164.310(a)(2)(iii), 164.310(b), 164.310(c), 164.310(d)(1), 164.310(d)(2)(iii), 164.312(b), 164.314(b)(2)(i)
		DE.CM-8: Vulnerability scans are performed	• COBIT 5 BAI03.10 • ISA 62443-2-1:2009 4.2.3.1, 4.2.3.7 • ISO/IEC 27001:2013 A.12.6.1 • NIST SP 800-53 Rev. 4 RA-5 • HIPAA Security Rule 45 C.F.R. §§ 164.308(a)(1)(i), 164.308(a)(8)
	Detection Processes (DE.DP): Detection processes and procedures are maintained and tested to ensure timely and adequate awareness of anomalous events.	**DE.DP-1:** Roles and responsibilities for detection are well defined to ensure accountability	• CCS CSC 5 • COBIT 5 DSS05.01 • ISA 62443-2-1:2009 4.4.3.1 • ISO/IEC 27001:2013 A.6.1.1 • NIST SP 800-53 Rev. 4 CA-2, CA-7, PM-14 • HIPAA Security Rule 45 C.F.R. §§ 164.308(a)(2), 164.308(a)(3)(ii)(A), 164.308(a)(3)(ii)(B), 164.308(a)(4), 164.310(a)(2)(iii), 164.312(a)(1), 164.312(a)(2)(ii)

Function	Category	Subcategory	Relevant Control Mappings[2]
		DE.DP-2: Detection activities comply with all applicable requirements	• ISA 62443-2-1:2009 4.4.3.2 • ISO/IEC 27001:2013 A.18.1.4 • NIST SP 800-53 Rev. 4 CA-2, CA-7, PM-14, SI-4 • HIPAA Security Rule 45 C.F.R. §§ 164.308(a)(1)(i), 164.308(a)(8)
		DE.DP-3: Detection processes are tested	• COBIT 5 APO13.02 • ISA 62443-2-1:2009 4.4.3.2 • ISA 62443-3-3:2013 SR 3.3 • ISO/IEC 27001:2013 A.14.2.8 • NIST SP 800-53 Rev. 4 CA-2, CA-7, PE-3, PM-14, SI-3, SI-4 • HIPAA Security Rule 45 C.F.R. § 164.306(e)
		DE.DP-4: Event detection information is communicated to appropriate parties	• COBIT 5 APO12.06 • ISA 62443-2-1:2009 4.3.4.5.9 • ISA 62443-3-3:2013 SR 6.1 • ISO/IEC 27001:2013 A.16.1.2 • NIST SP 800-53 Rev. 4 AU-6, CA-2, CA-7, RA-5, SI-4 • HIPAA Security Rule 45 C.F.R. §§ 164.308(a)(6)(ii), 164.314(a)(2)(i)(C), 164.314(a)(2)(iii)
		DE.DP-5: Detection processes are continuously improved	• COBIT 5 APO11.06, DSS04.05 • ISA 62443-2-1:2009 4.4.3.4 • ISO/IEC 27001:2013 A.16.1.6 • NIST SP 800-53 Rev. 4, CA-2, CA-7, PL-2, RA-5, SI-4, PM-14 • HIPAA Security Rule 45 C.F.R. §§ 164.306(e), 164.308(a)(8)

Function	Category	Subcategory	Relevant Control Mappings[2]
	Response Planning (RS.RP): Response processes and procedures are executed and maintained, to ensure timely response to detected cybersecurity events.	**RS.RP-1:** Response plan is executed during or after an event	• COBIT 5 BAI01.10 • CCS CSC 18 • ISA 62443-2-1:2009 4.3.4.5.1 • ISO/IEC 27001:2013 A.16.1.5 • NIST SP 800-53 Rev. 4 CP-2, CP-10, IR-4, IR-8 • HIPAA Security Rule 45 C.F.R. §§ 164.308(a)(6)(ii), 164.308(a)(7)(i), 164.308(a)(7)(ii)(A), 164.308(a)(7)(ii)(B), 164.308(a)(7)(ii)(C), 164.310(a)(2)(i), 164.312(a)(2)(ii)
	Communications (RS.CO): Response activities are coordinated with internal and external stakeholders, as appropriate, to include external support from law enforcement agencies.	**RS.CO-1:** Personnel know their roles and order of operations when a response is needed	• ISA 62443-2-1:2009 4.3.4.5.2, 4.3.4.5.3, 4.3.4.5.4 • ISO/IEC 27001:2013 A.6.1.1, A.16.1.1 • NIST SP 800-53 Rev. 4 CP-2, CP-3, IR-3, IR-8 • HIPAA Security Rule 45 C.F.R. §§ 164.308(a)(2), 164.308(a)(7)(ii)(A), 164.308(a)(7)(ii)(B), 164.308(a)(7)(ii)(C), 164.310(a)(2)(i), 164.308(a)(6)(i), 164.312(a)(2)(ii)
		RS.CO-2: Events are reported consistent with established criteria	• ISA 62443-2-1:2009 4.3.4.5.5 • ISO/IEC 27001:2013 A.6.1.3, A.16.1.2 • NIST SP 800-53 Rev. 4 AU-6, IR-6, IR-8 • HIPAA Security Rule 45 C.F.R. §§ 164.308(a)(5)(ii)(B), 164.308(a)(5)(ii)(C), 164.308(a)(6)(ii), 164.314(a)(2)(i)(C), 164.314(a)(2)(iii)

Function	Category	Subcategory	Relevant Control Mappings[2]
		RS.CO-3: Information is shared consistent with response plans	• ISA 62443-2-1:2009 4.3.4.5.2 • ISO/IEC 27001:2013 A.16.1.2 • NIST SP 800-53 Rev. 4 CA-2, CA-7, CP-2, IR-4, IR-8, PE-6, RA-5, SI-4 • HIPAA Security Rule 45 C.F.R. §§ 164.308(a)(5)(ii)(B), 164.308(a)(5)(ii)(C), 164.308(a)(6)(ii), 164.314(a)(2)(i)(C)
		RS.CO-4: Coordination with stakeholders occurs consistent with response plans	• ISA 62443-2-1:2009 4.3.4.5.5 • NIST SP 800-53 Rev. 4 CP-2, IR-4, IR-8 • HIPAA Security Rule 45 C.F.R. §§ 164.308(a)(6), 164.308(a)(7), 164.310(a)(2)(i), 164.312(a)(2)(ii)
		RS.CO-5: Voluntary information sharing occurs with external stakeholders to achieve broader cybersecurity situational awareness	• NIST SP 800-53 Rev. 4 PM-15, SI-5 • HIPAA Security Rule 45 C.F.R. § 164.308(a)(6)

Function	Category	Subcategory	Relevant Control Mappings[2]
	Analysis (RS.AN): Analysis is conducted to ensure adequate response and support recovery activities.	**RS.AN-1:** Notifications from detection systems are investigated	• COBIT 5 DSS02.07 • ISA 62443-2-1:2009 4.3.4.5.6, 4.3.4.5.7, 4.3.4.5.8 • ISA 62443-3-3:2013 SR 6.1 • ISO/IEC 27001:2013 A.12.4.1, A.12.4.3, A.16.1.5 • NIST SP 800-53 Rev. 4 AU-6, CA-7, IR-4, IR-5, PE-6, SI-4 • HIPAA Security Rule 45 C.F.R. §§ 164.308(a)(1)(i), 164.308(a)(1)(ii)(D), 164.308(a)(5)(ii)(B), 164.308(a)(5)(ii)(C), 164.308(a)(6)(ii), 164.312(b)
		RS.AN-2: The impact of the incident is understood	• ISA 62443-2-1:2009 4.3.4.5.6, 4.3.4.5.7, 4.3.4.5.8 • ISO/IEC 27001:2013 A.16.1.6 • NIST SP 800-53 Rev. 4 CP-2, IR-4 • HIPAA Security Rule 45 C.F.R. §§ 164.308(a)(6)(ii), 164.308(a)(7)(ii)(B), 164.308(a)(7)(ii)(C), 164.308(a)(7)(ii)(E)
		RS.AN-3: Forensics are performed	• ISA 62443-3-3:2013 SR 2.8, SR 2.9, SR 2.10, SR 2.11, SR 2.12, SR 3.9, SR 6.1 • ISO/IEC 27001:2013 A.16.1.7 • NIST SP 800-53 Rev. 4 AU-7, IR-4 • HIPAA Security Rule 45 C.F.R. § 164.308(a)(6)
RESPOND (RS)		**RS.AN-4:** Incidents are categorized consistent with response plans	• ISA 62443-2-1:2009 4.3.4.5.6 • ISO/IEC 27001:2013 A.16.1.4 • NIST SP 800-53 Rev. 4 CP-2, IR-4, IR-5, IR-8 • HIPAA Security Rule 45 C.F.R. § 164.308(a)(6)(ii)

Function	Category	Subcategory	Relevant Control Mappings[2]
	Mitigation (RS.MI): Activities are performed to prevent expansion of an event, mitigate its effects, and eradicate the incident.	**RS.MI-1:** Incidents are contained	• ISA 62443-2-1:2009 4.3.4.5.6 • ISA 62443-3-3:2013 SR 5.1, SR 5.2, SR 5.4 • ISO/IEC 27001:2013 A.16.1.5 • NIST SP 800-53 Rev. 4 IR-4 • HIPAA Security Rule 45 C.F.R. § 164.308(a)(6)(ii)
		RS.MI-2: Incidents are mitigated	• ISA 62443-2-1:2009 4.3.4.5.6, 4.3.4.5.10 • ISO/IEC 27001:2013 A.12.2.1, A.16.1.5 • NIST SP 800-53 Rev. 4 IR-4 • HIPAA Security Rule 45 C.F.R. § 164.308(a)(6)(ii)
		RS.MI-3: Newly identified vulnerabilities are mitigated or documented as accepted risks	• ISO/IEC 27001:2013 A.12.6.1 • NIST SP 800-53 Rev. 4 CA-7, RA-3, RA-5 • HIPAA Security Rule 45 C.F.R. §§ 164.308(a)(1)(ii)(A), 164.308(a)(1)(ii)(B), 164.308(a)(6)(ii)
	Improvements (RS.IM): Organizational response activities are improved by incorporating lessons learned from current and previous detection/response activities.	**RS.IM-1:** Response plans incorporate lessons learned	• COBIT 5 BAI01.13 • ISA 62443-2-1:2009 4.3.4.5.10, 4.4.3.4 • ISO/IEC 27001:2013 A.16.1.6 • NIST SP 800-53 Rev. 4 CP-2, IR-4, IR-8 • HIPAA Security Rule 45 C.F.R. §§ 164.308(a)(7)(ii)(D), 164.308(a)(8), 164.316(b)(2)(iii)
		RS.IM-2: Response strategies are updated	• NIST SP 800-53 Rev. 4 CP-2, IR-4, IR-8 • HIPAA Security Rule 45 C.F.R. §§ 164.308(a)(7)(ii)(D), 164.308(a)(8)
Recovery Planning (RC.RP): Recovery		**RC.RP-1:** Recovery	• CCS CSC 8

Function	Category	Subcategory	Relevant Control Mappings[2]
	processes and procedures are executed and maintained to ensure timely restoration of systems or assets affected by cybersecurity events.	plan is executed during or after an event	• COBIT 5 DSS02.05, DSS03.04 • ISO/IEC 27001:2013 A.16.1.5 • NIST SP 800-53 Rev. 4 CP-10, IR-4, IR-8 • HIPAA Security Rule 45 C.F.R. §§ 164.308(a)(7), 164.310(a)(2)(i)
	Improvements (RC.IM): Recovery planning and processes are improved by incorporating lessons learned into future activities.	**RC.IM-1:** Recovery plans incorporate lessons learned	• COBIT 5 BAI05.07 • ISA 62443-2-1:2009 4.4.3.4 • NIST SP 800-53 Rev. 4 CP-2, IR-4, IR-8 • HIPAA Security Rule 45 C.F.R. §§ 164.308(a)(7)(ii)(D), 164.308(a)(8), 164.316(b)(2)(iii)
RECOVER (RC)		**RC.IM-2:** Recovery strategies are updated	• COBIT 5 BAI07.08 • NIST SP 800-53 Rev. 4 CP-2, IR-4, IR-8 • HIPAA Security Rule 45 C.F.R. §§ 164.308(a)(7)(ii)(D), 164.308(a)(8)
	Communications (RC.CO): Restoration activities are coordinated with internal and external parties, such as coordinating centers, Internet Service Providers, owners of attacking systems, victims, other CSIRTs, and	**RC.CO-1:** Public relations are managed	• COBIT 5 EDM03.02 • HIPAA Security Rule 45 C.F.R. § 164.308(a)(6)(i)[5]
		RC.CO-2: Reputation after an event is repaired	• COBIT 5 EDM03.02 • HIPAA Security Rule 45 C.F.R. § 164.308(a)(6)(i)[5]

---

[5] Although public relations management and reputation repair are not specifically required by the HIPAA Security Rule's Security Incident Procedures standard (45 C.F.R. § 164.308(a)(6)(i)), HIPAA covered entities and business associates may implement such procedures as components of their compliance activities.

Function	Category	Subcategory	Relevant Control Mappings[2]
	vendors.	**RC.CO-3:** Recovery activities are communicated to internal stakeholders and executive and management teams	• NIST SP 800-53 Rev. 4 CP-2, IR-4 • HIPAA Security Rule 45 C.F.R. §§ 164.308(a)(6)(ii), 164.308(a)(7)(ii)(B), 164.308(a)(7)(ii)(C), 164.310(a)(2)(i), 164.314(a)(2)(i)(C)

DHHS Office for Civil Rights | *HIPAA Security Rule Crosswalk to NIST Cybersecurity Framework*

21972800R00037

Printed in Great Britain
by Amazon